The PRAYERFUL *Spirit*

PASSION FOR GOD,
COMPASSION FOR PEOPLE

The PRAYERFUL Spirit

Passion for God, Compassion for People

By James P. Gills, M.D.

THE PRAYERFUL SPIRIT by James P. Gills, M.D.
Published by Creation House Press
A Part of Strang Communications Company
600 Rinehart Road
Lake Mary, FL 32746
www.creationhouse.com

Unless otherwise noted, the Scripture quotations are from The Holy Bible, New International Version. Copyright © 1973, 1978, 1984 by the International Bible Society. Used by permission of Zondervan Publishing House. All rights reserved.

Cover design by Rachel Campbell
Interior design by David Bilby

Library of Congress Control Number: 2003101123
International Standard Book Number: 1-59185-215-3

03 04 05 06 07 — 8 7 6 5 4 3 2 1
Printed in the United States of America

This book is dedicated to all of us as we joyfully align ourselves to our Savior and to His work.

Acknowledgments

This book would not have been possible without the inspiration and encouragement of many people. First I would like to thank all those who contributed their time, energy and thoughts about prayer: Dr. William Farr Andrews of Germantown, Tennessee; Dr. James A. Avery of Clearwater, Florida; Dr. Juan F. Batlle of Santo Domingo, Dominican Republic; Dr. Henry Brandt of Riviera Beach, Florida; Dr. Jack C. Cooper of Dallas, Texas; Dr. Dennis Cox of New Port Richey, Florida; Chaplain Ralph A. Curtis of St. Petersburg, Florida; Dr. Timothy N. Daley of Palm Harbor, Florida; Mickey Evans of the Dunklin Memorial Camp, Okeechobee, Florida; Dr. Hal E. Furr of Salisbury, North Carolina; Dr. Lowell A. Gess of Alexandria, Minnesota; Dr. Tom Goodgame of Clearwater, Florida; Dr. William Hale of Clearwater, Florida; the late Dr. William H. Havener; Dr. Ronald E. Haynes of Palm Harbor, Florida; Dr. Ralph E. Johnson of St. Petersburg, Florida; Dr. Peter Knight of Tampa, Florida; Dr. Gerald E. Lane of Gardner, Kansas; Dr. John McCormick of Toronto; Dr. Dan G. Montgomery of Inverness, Florida; Dr. James B. Morris of Palm Harbor, Florida; Dr. Robert H. Osher of Cincinnati, Ohio; Dr. Walter Tuck Parkerson of Charlotte, North Carolina; Dr. Walter J. Paschall of Tyler, Texas; Dr. William Standish Reed of Tampa, Florida; Dr. David P. Sloan Jr., of Leesburg, Florida; Dr. Al Thomas of Hot Springs, Arkansas; Dr. Spencer Thornton of Nashville, Tennessee; Dr. Elizabeth Vaughn of Dallas, Texas; and Dr. John V. Verner of Plant City, Florida.

I would like to extend a special thanks to Dr. J. James Rowsey, of St. Luke's Cataract and Laser Institute, and to Dr. J. Lawton Smith. Jim has provided a special inspiration as I have worked on this book, and Lawton has given me direction and advice that I hope benefits not only myself but those who read these pages.

The lives of all these doctors give testimony to the power of God and the special relationship each of us can have with

vii

Him through prayer. The blessings He has bestowed on these doctors and their patients bear witness to His greatness and grace.

The staff members at St. Luke's Cataract and Laser Institute generously have provided much encouragement and direction.

David A. Seamands, the author of numerous books about Christians in recovery, has given much advice through hours of discussion on this important topic.

And a special thanks to my wife, Heather. Her ceaseless love and insight help me see more clearly the heart of God.

Contents

PROLOGUE

Every morning when I wake up, my eyes focus on a plaque with a quote from Mother Teresa of Calcutta. It says, "A life not lived for others is not worth living." It is a reminder of my constant objective: to be faithful, fervent and focused first in my relationship with God and then in my relationships with others.

To me, those three Fs are vitally important. They help me balance my spiritual life with the reality of the world in which we live. They help me as I make choices every day about whether to honor and serve my Redeemer. They help me set my priorities in every area of my life— my work, my family, my friends—so that I keep the Lord first and am in the habit of turning to Christ every day, every moment, whether waking or sleeping.

But how do I do that? The key is prayer—not just the rote prayer I learned as a child—but a deep, rich, full, meaningful relationship with my Creator and Redeemer. Intimate communication with the Lord through prayer gives me a feeling that God understands. I know that He surrounds me with His presence. Andrew Bonar, a key figure in the revivals in Scotland in the 1840s, tells us to "measure your days by what you've accomplished in prayer." Prayer is the means by which I stay faithful, fervent and focused.

I start my day by focusing on the blessings I have received. The first of these is my wife, Heather. Every morning I ask the Lord to bless each part of her body. I pray that He will bless her head and mouth, her arms and hands, her heart and lungs, her legs and feet. I ask for Heather's whole being to be lifted up as a blessing to and from God. And she does the same with me. Throughout my day, I thank God for all the blessings He has bestowed on me, and I praise His name. As Psalm 71:8 says, "My mouth is filled with your praise, declaring your splendor all day long."

One morning this spring, we sat for an entire hour contemplating how difficult it is to pray. We simply turned to the Scriptures and read the twenty-third Psalm. The concept of the Lord being our shepherd was more than we could grasp. Everything in our environment tells us to be productive and to make decisions, but the Lord tells us to be quiet and to let His words guide our actions.

There are times when I dry up and forget to pray; times when I am too busy to spend that hour in prayer. Those are the times when I lose focus and things begin to go wrong. Prayer is the way of living through our problems. We do not have to tackle every problem on our own—when we pray, we are reminded that God is with us.

The Scriptures tell us that unceasing prayer will change our lives. As my faith walk with the Lord has matured, those changes have been revealed to me in many areas—my marriage, my family and, most definitely, in my work and my relationships with patients.

My colleagues' experiences with prayer have helped shape my own spiritual journey and the ideas I share in this book. I have asked some of them to share their experiences in their own prayer lives and as they pray with their patients and others.

Doctors know a lot about commitment when it comes to work. They have committed to long hours and are dedicated to their patients. Making that kind of commitment to prayer doesn't seem as productive.

Prayer is tough. It is easier to put money in the plate; it is easier to tithe; it is easier to work for the Lord; it is easier to be a missionary or a pastor than to pray and pray unceasingly.

But as shown by my colleagues' stories, prayer gives us access to the power of God. People are healed and lives are changed. Prayer aligns us with God and gives us greater peace, joy and fulfillment than anything we could seek.

Part One

The Priority of Prayer

Chapter One

What Is Prayer?

Be still and know that I am God.
—Psalm 46:10

To you, O Lord, I lift up my soul; in you I trust, O my God
—Psalm 25:1

Prayer is a conversation of the heart with God. Through prayer we align ourselves with our Creator, and His presence is revealed to us. We grow in our love and worship of Him. And when we are united with our Lord through prayer, our lives become fuller, richer, more joyous and more peaceful.

Having a spirit of prayer is one of the most important factors in our walk with Christ. We must be meditative and contemplative while listening to Him speak. Then our lives are changed. When we pray in the Spirit, we are in prayer in our whole life, not just our "prayer" time. We are praying as we work, as we play, as we spend time alone and as we spend time with friends and family.

"A good prayer life, in my estimation, is being aware of God's presence and being transparent with Him about what I am experiencing," says Dr. Dennis Cox of New Port Richey, Florida. "Sometimes that involves a formal audible prayer, but more often it is a thought life that is shared with God."

I heard a pastor in Clearwater, Florida, recently talk about our godly relationships. He said the only thing we'll be judged on is how we relate to others on a godly basis. We need to ask ourselves whether our relationships at work and at home are godly. Prayer helps us examine our relationship with our Creator and helps

us focus our relationships with others so they indeed
are godly.

For prayer helps us know the heart of our Lord and
His desires for our lives. I heard an interesting statement: "We see what we are programmed to see." In
other words, we set our minds so we get out of things
only what we want to get out of them.

But when we are constantly seeking our Lord in
prayer, we align ourselves with His wishes and desires.
We are no longer programmed to see what we want, but
we see what God wants. We turn over control of our
lives to Him and do His will. In prayer we pour out to
Him our joys, our anguish and petitions for others and
ourselves. And by faith we know He hears and
responds to our cries.

Leonard Ravenhill has written, "Prayer must have
priority. Prayer must be our bolt to lock up the night,
our key to open the day." Prayer is the single most
important action we can take to know God, to be in
union with Him. If we don't have a good prayer life, our
priorities get mixed up.

Charles H. Spurgeon, a nineteenth-century Baptist
minister in England, once asked:

> Why is it that some people are often in a place of
> worship and yet they're not holy? It is because
> they neglect their [prayer] closets. They love the
> wheat, but they do not grind it; they would have
> the corn, but they will not go forth into the field
> to gather it; the fruit hangs on the tree, but they
> will not pluck it; and the water flows at their feet,
> but they'll not stoop to drink it.

If we neglect our prayer life, we lose sight of our Lord,
and we become proud and arrogant people who think we
don't need God. Prayer, therefore, sets us straight and
keeps us safe in our Lord.

> The LORD is my rock, my fortress and my deliverer;

> my God is my rock, in whom I take refuge. He is my
> shield and the horn of my salvation, my stronghold.
>   —PSALM 18:2

How we view God and pray to Him indicates where our priorities are and whether we have the privilege of realizing that God belongs above and ahead of everything.

Prayer exerts unbelievable demands on us. As we open our hearts and allow the Lord to rule our lives, He will develop us in ways far beyond anything we, on our own, have ever attempted. Worshipful prayer transcends the structure of ingrained behavior and rigid church traditions. In prayer we can experience the holy and compassionate heart of the Lord.

LOVE AND PRAYER

The essence of praying as we should is spelled out in Matthew 22:34–40:

> Hearing that Jesus had silenced the Sadducees, the Pharisees got together. One of them, an expert in the law, tested him with this question: "Teacher, which is the greatest commandment in the Law?"
>
> Jesus replied: "'Love the Lord your God with all your heart and with all your soul and with all your mind.' This is the first and greatest commandment. And the second is like it: 'Love your neighbor as yourself.' All the Law and the Prophets hang on these two commandments."

Our Lord commands a relationship of love with Him, reflected in our prayer lives. Without love, our prayers are meaningless, a series of empty words. Without love, our walk with God is a ritual. Without love, we cannot truly know and worship Him. But when we approach God in love, our prayers are a rich, full experience. He seeks a relationship of love and adoration so we can talk together and have Him with us at all times.

Robert J. Sternberg, a professor of psychology and education at Yale, says intimacy, commitment and passion make up a "love triangle" between two people. In a 1987 article in *Prevention* magazine he describes how the three parts affect the relationship of love.

We can extend this triangle to our relationship with God. Perfect balance among these three elements helps us achieve the highest form of love. But what do we mean by intimacy, commitment and passion with God?

The first side of the triangle is intimacy or "knowing." In both Hebrew and Greek, "to know" implies an intimate relationship best seen in a very close friendship. It is a relationship that takes time and effort. An intimate relationship is built and strengthened by sharing ideas and experiences, by support, communication and warmth. One soul opens up to another, building comradeship and mutual dependence that lend support in times of trouble. The two people are aligned in their daily relationship and in their hopes and dreams for the future.

To become intimate with God, we need to know the Word and the person of Jesus Christ. If we're just acquainted with Him, we know about the God of creation, but we certainly don't love Him. It is merely an awareness of someone we don't know on an intimate basis. To "know" God, we need to study His Word faithfully on a regular basis and to seek His true blessings on us in His intimacy. We then know His will for our lives and can turn to Him in times of trouble as well as in times of joy.

The second side of the triangle is our commitment to Him. Commitment provides the reliable strength necessary for the relationship to survive the ups and downs of our lives on earth. It's where the decision to love and maintain love is made. Commitment will grow or wither depending on how it is nurtured.

Proverbs 16:3 says, "Commit to the Lord whatever you do, and your plans will succeed." One way we help commitment grow is by staying focused on God through prayer. As Psalm 34:1 says, "I will extol the Lord at all times; his praise will always be on my lips."

But we must make sure we're committed to more than the habit of prayer. We must seek to be focused, fervent and faithful in our relationship to our Redeemer.

The third side in our triangle relationship of love with God is passion. Romance and physical union between husband and wife are essential components for fulfilling love. Passion makes spouses desire to be united. And passion motivates them to greater commitment and leads to deeper intimacy with one another.

Just as passion cements the marriage relationship, so it should seal our relationship with God. We should pray deeply and passionately, making God our highest priority, above all other concerns and desires. This passion motivates us to put Him first.

In my life as a physician, having passion for the Lord and compassion for my patients go hand in hand. I have failed in this pursuit many times, and the Lord in His mercy repeatedly has shown me that my compassion for patients must come from the passion I have for Him.

All three facets of this love relationship play a vital role in our prayer lives. If they are balanced and work together, our lives are focused on God, and we have set Him as the highest priority. We know Him and study His Word, we are committed to a life of prayer, and we pray fervently, not as a task to be accomplished but because we desire a closer relationship with Him. We know God and we love Him. That really determines whether we pray to Him. We want to align ourselves with our Creator and put Him as our highest priority, far above the material things of this world.

THE STRUGGLE TO PRAY

That's not to say life is easy even when we are focused on the Lord through prayer. We still will face problems, frustrations and difficult times. But some of the most difficult events in our lives are meant to help us rely on God. Just as Calvary was the worst day in the world, it also was the best day. Our worst events will make us the strongest, because when we rely on the Lord instead of collapsing, we turn all our attention to Him and not to ourselves. We seek God's way, rather than our own.

Even though we are assured countless blessings through our relationship with our Lord in prayer, we still struggle to do it. Prayer is not natural. It is easier to contribute time or money than to pray and to pray unceasingly.

Prayer also interferes with our ambitions and our own agendas. It forces us to surrender our independence and submit to God. The only thing He asks of us is to trust in His grace and then to grow closer to Him. It sounds simple, but living that commitment every day requires constant dedication. God renews and renourishes that commitment in us through our contact with Him in prayer.

Some days, when complications pile up or my schedule gets bogged down, I question the purpose of my work. Prayer is the only way out of those dark situations. When I remember that the only work that makes a difference is the work done for the Lord, I am reminded of my need to turn to Him.

WHY SHOULD WE PRAY?

We know that prayer reveals the heart of God, that we have a relationship of love reflected in our prayer and that, even though we face problems and don't feel like praying, prayer is essential. We need the presence of God in our lives, and prayer helps us align ourselves with Him.

There are three stages we go through in prayer that

help show us its purpose—prayer honors God, prayer aligns us to God and prayer meets our needs. Each of these helps build our relationship of love with our Lord.

PRAYER HONORS GOD

> The LORD is my light and my salvation—whom shall I fear? The LORD is the stronghold of my life—of whom shall I be afraid?
>
> —PSALM 27:1

First, in our prayer we should honor God. Arthur W. Pink, in *Profiting From the Word*, says, "Prayer is an act of worship, a paying homage" to our Father in heaven. The Scriptures are full of verses that show us how to honor God, how to worship and praise Him.

> Prayer cannot be successfully separated from worship, for it prepares the soul for worship, expresses the spirit in worship and interacts with God, which is worship. Worship without prayer is like daytime without light, a school without students, a choir without music, or an automobile without fuel...the praying saint cannot keep from worshiping; the prayerless saint cannot rise to worship.
>
> —JUDSON CORNWALL

We must get serious about worship if we want a lifestyle of prayer. How can we pray to God if we don't first acknowledge Him as our Redeemer and Lord? In worship, as in prayer, we align ourselves with God.

PRAYER ALIGNS US TO GOD

Second, through prayer we become "inclined to God," humbling ourselves so we become totally dependent on Him and we seek His will in all we do every day and in every decision of our lives.

A lifestyle of prayer leads us to the realization that without Him we can do nothing of lasting value. The apostle Paul recognized his helplessness without God, writing in Romans 7:18, "I know that nothing good lives in me, that is, in my sinful nature. For I have the desire to do what is good, but I cannot carry it out."

When we're not in touch with God through prayer, we think we can take care of ourselves when we can't. We think we're independent and in control of our lives. Funny thing, the more we pray, the more we realize how dependent upon God we are. Those times when I'm too busy to pray, the wheel falls off my car. Soon, I'm spinning toward a crash. Life ceases to be a joy. We need the Lord more than we realize. James 4:10 says, "Humble yourselves before the Lord, and he will lift you up."

By making God our highest priority, we acknowledge that He is in control and that we want to align ourselves with Him in every decision we make and every action we take.

> Seek first his kingdom and his righteousness, and
> all these things will be given to you as well.
> —MATTHEW 6:33

Every time we do something, we have a choice. We have a choice to do it as the world does it, or as the Lord Jesus would have us do it. In prayer we discover what He wants us to do. We learn to open ourselves to Him, seek His will, and depend on His guidance and love.

The worst thing I can do as a physician is seek applause and acceptance from men rather than seek to please God. It is far easier for physicians with large practices to worship the rewards, financially and emotionally, from our patients. It's tempting to want to be worshiped as a physician and to worship the job rather than worship the Lord. Instead, the challenge, the struggle, is to want to serve Jesus through our surrender to His will. Then we can serve others with humility and an attitude of caring and love.

Prayer Meets Our Needs

> Ask, and it will be given to you; seek and you will find; knock and the door will be opened to you. For everyone who asks receives; he who seeks finds; and to him who knocks, the door will be opened.
>
> —Matthew 7:7–8

> You may ask me for anything in my name, and I will do it.
>
> —John 14:14

The third reason for prayer is so we may receive what we need from God. He gives us what we need, in line with His character. When we ask of God in the name of Jesus, we pray for the same things He desires to give us, as outlined in His Word.

Prayer, therefore, involves agreeing with God—being aligned with Him. We direct our prayers toward the accomplishment of His purposes in this world. Praying God's promises ensures victory and God's blessings upon us.

> "For I know the plans I have for you," declares the LORD, "plans to prosper you and not to harm you, plans to give you hope and a future. Then you will call upon me and come and pray to me, and I will listen to you. You will seek me and find me when you seek me with all your heart."
>
> —Jeremiah 29:11–13

In Conclusion

Prayer helps us make sure we are constantly focused on our Redeemer and Lord. Our prayer as Christians should be to seek to be with Christ, worshiping Him on the cross. It should be faithful, fervent and focused, consuming all the facets of our lives. Our job is to integrate our whole life with Christ—our work, our play, our families—so that everything we do, every choice we make, is based on our subconscious awareness of the person of Jesus Christ.

A life of prayer develops the life of God in each of us; it doesn't develop ourselves or promote our motives. But it does change us as we come closer to Him. We grow more dependent on God, more faithful to Him, and we love Him and others more as we spend more time in prayer.

Prayer in Action

Chapter One: What Is Prayer?

For group discussion or personal reflection:

1. What does it mean to align yourself with God? How can you do it in your life?

2. What are some specific examples in your life of the changes prayer has brought about?

3. Why do you need to pray?

4. How are the elements of the love triangle—intimacy, commitment, and passion—reflected in your prayer life?

5. What can make it difficult for you to pray?

6. Think about a time in your life when you didn't pray regularly. What happened?

7. What do we get from God when we pray? What have you personally received from Him?

Chapter Two

PREPARING TO PRAY

May the words of my mouth and the meditation of my heart
be pleasing in your sight, O LORD, my Rock and my Redeemer.
—PSALM 19:14

A study of the meditative lifestyles of some believers reveals the ample time they set aside to live close to God and to listen to Him. John Wesley, the British founder of Methodism, described how he was able to achieve this: "Though I am always in haste, I am never in a hurry because I never undertake more work than I can go through with calmness of spirit."

To develop a lifestyle of prayer in our lives, we need to have that same calmness of spirit. To achieve this, we must first prepare our hearts and minds for prayer. We wouldn't think of going on a long car trip without checking the map to see where we're going, packing what we'll need, and making sure our car is in working condition and has a full tank of gas.

In the same way, we need to prepare ourselves for prayer. Our road map is God's Word. We should study it to know God's promises and direction for our lives. We should have no excess baggage on our trip, which means we need to clear away any distractions so we can focus fully on aligning ourselves with our Redeemer in prayer. And to make sure we're in working condition, we need to clean our thoughts, have the right attitude for prayer and have the right relationship with God and others.

KNOW GOD'S WORD

Do not let this Book of the Law depart from your mouth; meditate on it day and night, so that you

may be careful to do everything written in it.
Then you will be prosperous and successful.

—JOSHUA 1:8

The Word of God must permeate every aspect of our lives in order for us to be able to pray. And God commands us, along with Joshua, to learn His Word and speak it in prayer to receive His blessings. By learning His Word, we learn about our Creator and Redeemer. We know His will for us, His expectations for us, and His love and grace. We see Him more clearly, and we align our thoughts and wishes with His.

God wants us to know Him in a personal relationship built through prayer. He doesn't want us just to do good works or contribute time or money. If we do those things without a close relationship with our Redeemer, we're not doing His will. God knows the desires of our hearts, and He wants us to hunger after His presence.

Reading God's Word as part of the time we set aside to pray also helps focus that time on God, not on ourselves or worldly distractions. When we study His Word, we put God as our top priority and we want to be united with Him through prayer.

CLEAR AWAY DISTRACTIONS

Be still before the LORD and wait patiently for him.

—PSALM 37:7

When we're in prayer with God, we need to be focused solely on Him—to "be still" as the psalmist says, seeking to hear His voice in our lives. As we develop our lifestyle of prayer, we strive to focus our thoughts on our Redeemer all the time. (We'll talk later about building this kind of relationship.) To stay focused, we need to deal with the distractions that are bound to crop up and affect our relationship with God.

One way to deal with distractions is to set aside special

times during our day committed solely to prayer.
Schedule other tasks and appointments around that time.
Unplug the phone and don't answer the door. Give that
time to God alone. A time of solitude allows us to bring
our whole being to the Lord; to empty ourselves mentally;
to seek only Him.

CLEAN OUR THOUGHTS

Whatever is true, whatever is noble, whatever is
right, whatever is pure, whatever is lovely, whatever is admirable—if anything is excellent or
praiseworthy—think about such things.

—PHILIPPIANS 4:8

Before we pray, we need to clean our thoughts, taking
time to wash away every thought of the world and its
agendas—to let our minds be at rest. We can't be focusing
our thoughts on Him when we're worried about problems
at work or at home. We are to bring our cares and concerns to God in prayer—not let them keep us from Him.
If we allow those issues to clutter our minds, we won't be
able to seek His will and listen for His guidance.

Then, once we've handed those concerns to the Lord,
we need to fill our minds with the Holy Spirit. We should
have the beauty of a clean mind that can think well for
the Lord.

HAVE THE RIGHT MOTIVES

To some who were confident of their own righteousness and looked down on everybody else,
Jesus told this parable: "Two men went up to the
temple to pray, one a Pharisee and the other a tax
collector. The Pharisee stood up and prayed about
himself: 'God, I thank you that I am not like other
men—robbers, evildoers, adulterers—or even like
this tax collector. I fast twice a week and give a
tenth of all I get.' But the tax collector stood at a
distance. He would not even look up to heaven,

but beat his breast and said, 'God, have mercy on me, a sinner.' I tell you that this man, rather than the other, went home justified before God. For everyone who exalts himself will be humbled, and he who humbles himself will be exalted."

—LUKE 18:9–14

In prayer, as in everything, our motives are very important. If we ask for things to please ourselves or impress others, we have the wrong motives. If we're after what we can get for ourselves, rather than being surrendered to God and His will, our prayers are not proper. As James 4:3 says, "When you ask, you do not receive, because you ask with wrong motives that you may spend what you get on your pleasures."

Often we really want God to be something He is not. There is a God we want and a God who is, and they are not the same. Many times we don't understand God. As Isaiah 55:8 says, "'For my thoughts are not your thoughts, neither are your ways my ways,' declares the Lord." It is through prayer that we begin to bridge the gap, to get a glimpse of who God is and who He wants us to be.

Therefore, in our prayer life, we need a proper gaze, focused on Jesus Christ. If we allow our gaze to be on our requests, those requests will consume us. We end up telling God what we need to be done; we attempt to control Him.

But the Lord is not a servant or an errand boy responding to our wishes. If He gave us everything we ask for—to live longer, to get rid of nearsightedness, to own a bigger house—we'd be satisfied with this world and we wouldn't look forward to being with Him in heaven. The reason for our salvation is not to be saved from our problems but to be saved from our selfishness. Selfishness is more than behavior. When we're selfish, we focus on our own wants and needs. When we're selfless, we're inclined to God. It's the selfish who demand, and they're miserable. It's the selfless who give, and they become close to Christ. The selfish keep wondering what the selfless are talking about, for they never understand.

As we said earlier, one of the reasons we pray is to receive from God. He wants to provide for us, but He also wants our thoughts and motives in line with His will.

So we pray to God Almighty as our Redeemer and Savior, seeking His will in our lives and having faith that He will provide for our every need. Psalm 37:4 assures us of this: "Delight yourself in the Lord and he will give you the desires of your heart."

If our prayers were answered for the wrong reasons, we would continue to come to God for what we get from Him. We would continue to pray so we could gain material goods. Our selfishness would be fed, and we wouldn't recognize that we should surrender our will to God.

When we ask of God, we should ask in His name for His will to be done. Jesus tells us in John 16:23–24, "I tell you the truth, my Father will give you whatever you ask in my name. Until now you have not asked for anything in my name. Ask and you will receive, and your joy will be complete."

When we do that, we hand Him our selfishness, our desire for control, our desire for worldly possessions. We have a feeling of love that is a result of God redeeming us from our sins.

Does prayer change events? It may. But the most important effect of prayer is that it changes the person who is praying to become more like the One to whom he is praying—our Redeemer.

> Dear friends, if our hearts do not condemn us, we have confidence before God and receive from him anything we ask, because we obey his commands and do what pleases him.
>
> —1 JOHN 3:21–22

SEEK GOD'S FORGIVENESS

But your iniquities have separated you from your
God; your sins have hidden his face from you, so
that he will not hear.

—ISAIAH 59:2

In the same way that we clean our thoughts and make
sure we have the right motives in prayer, we also must
clean our hearts of sin against our Lord. If we try to pray,
but try to hide sin from Him, we create a wall that prayer
cannot overcome.

We must be prepared to be honest with God, to confess our sins and our weaknesses. He knows them
already. But in being honest with our Lord, we seek
reunion with Him and can be made whole with Him
again. Psalm 66:18–19 says, "If I had cherished sin in my
heart, the Lord would not have listened; but God has
surely listened and heard my voice in prayer."

We must clear away any stumbling blocks that would
isolate us from Him and be prepared to ask, and receive,
His forgiveness for our sins.

FORGIVE OTHERS

Anyone who claims to be in the light, but hates
his brother is still in the darkness.

—1 JOHN 2:9

In the same way that we reconcile our relationship
with God, we must reconcile our relationships with
others. And just as God forgives our sins, so we must forgive others. Mark 11:25 says, "And when you stand
praying, if you hold anything against anyone, forgive him,
so that your Father in heaven may forgive you your sins."

The greatest part of prayer is to forgive others.
Righteousness, which is the ultimate aspect of the
Christian walk, is impossible to achieve until we have
been forgiven and in turn forgive. Unless we forgive, we

can never be in a true relationship with the Lord and live according to His purposes.

In Conclusion

To prepare ourselves for prayer we must be ready to listen to our Redeemer. It takes time, effort and practice to put the distractions of the world—work, hectic schedules, families—on hold so we can study His Word and seek Him.

We also must always put ourselves on the line to have an open, honest and joyous relationship with God in prayer. We have to be vigilant in making sure our motives are aligned with God's motives. And we must be honest with Him about the sins that keep us from being inclined to Him. In the same way, we must have open relationships with others. It can be hard work, but the benefits far outweigh the risks.

> Therefore we do not lose heart. Though outwardly we are wasting away, yet inwardly we are being renewed day by day. For our light and momentary troubles are achieving for us an eternal glory that far outweighs them all. So we fix our eyes not on what is seen, but on what is unseen. For what is seen is temporary, but what is unseen is eternal.
>
> —2 Corinthians 4:16–18

PRAYER IN ACTION

CHAPTER TWO: PREPARING TO PRAY

For group discussion or personal reflection:

1. How can you include God's Word in your prayer life?

2. What are some ways for you to set aside time for prayer? Do you really not have time to pray?

3. What are the right motives for you to pray? The wrong motives? How do you know the difference?

4. What are some ways you can be selfless, rather than selfish, in prayer?

5. Do you try to hide your sins from God? How can you practice being honest with Him and seeking His forgiveness and grace?

6. Are there some things for which you can't forgive others? How often do you carry a grudge?

7. If we're praying to God, why do we need to worry about our relationships with other people? Does that affect your ability to pray?

Chapter Three

PUTTING GOD FIRST

Whaat we know of God affects how we pray. To have a deep, meaningful relationship with Him, we need to see Him as our Lord and Savior. In the last chapter, we talked about the importance of knowing God's Word and speaking it in prayer. And when we are full of the Word, we are full of the Holy Spirit. The two work together to bring us closer to God and to align us with Him.

The following verses help give us a fuller picture of our Creator and Redeemer, and they show us how we should give Him priority in our lives. When we are aligned with God, we give Him the proper priority and are able to pray to Him as we ought.

OUR FOUNDATION

Believe in the Lord Jesus and you will be saved—
you and your household.

—ACTS 16:31

Paul and Silas tell the jailer holding them prisoner what he must do to be saved. All of us must see Jesus as the foundation in our lives—the basis for all the choices and decisions we make. This brings a change in our lives. We no longer live according to what we want to do, but we seek His will because we put Him at the center of our lives. We want to do His will.

OUR LIFEGIVER

I am the vine; you are the branches. If a man remains in me and I in him, he will bear much fruit.

—JOHN 15:5

Jesus tells us we must abide in Him; we must surrender our agendas and desires and align our whole being toward Christ the Vine. Branches cannot act independently if they are to produce any fruit; they must grow from the main vine. Therefore, we must give up our independence and rely on Christ.

Our Lord

He restores my soul. He guides me in the paths of righteousness for his name's sake.

—PSALM 23:3

Christ is our Lord. When we obey Him we bring honor and glory to Him and show others that we believe. In the New Testament, Paul sets the standard for how we show Him that we believe in Him as our Lord:

Then Paul answered, "Why are you weeping and breaking my heart? I am ready not only to be bound, but also to die in Jerusalem for the name of the Lord Jesus."

—ACTS 21:13

Therefore, I urge you, brothers, in view of God's mercy, to offer your bodies as living sacrifices, holy and pleasing to God—this is your spiritual act of worship.

—ROMANS 12:1

Christ died for us. We must be ready to die and live for Him.

Our Beloved

If we live, we live to the Lord; and if we die, we die to the Lord. So, whether we live or die, we belong to the Lord. For this very reason, Christ died and returned to life so that he might be the Lord of both the dead and the living.

—ROMANS 14:8–9

> And he died for all, that those who live should no
> longer live for themselves but for him who died
> for them and was raised again.
>
> —2 Corinthians 5:15

> So whether you eat or drink or whatever you do,
> do it all for the glory of God.
>
> —1 Corinthians 10:31

All the aspects of our lives, and our lives themselves, belong to Christ, who gave up His own life for us. We commit our lives to Him because we love Him, and we build a relationship of love through prayer. As we discussed earlier, He seeks that relationship of love so we can have Him with us at all times. And when we love Him, our actions are guided by that love. Therefore, we live our lives for Jesus. All the parts of our lives—marriage, work, and lifestyle—should then honor the One we love.

Our Model

> Dear friends, now we are children of God, and
> what we will be has not yet been made known.
> But we know that when he appears, we shall be
> like him, for we shall see him as he is.
>
> —1 John 3:2

Our "marriage" with Christ will transform us. We shall be intimate with Him, be like Him and know Him.

> For those God foreknew he also predestined to be
> conformed to the likeness of his Son, that he
> might be the firstborn among many brothers.
>
> —Romans 8:29

In many facets of our lives we become like what we love. So it is in our love relationship with Christ. We become like Him when we love Him.

OUR SECRET

> For you died, and your life is now hidden with
> Christ in God.
>
> —COLOSSIANS 3:3

When we turn our lives over to Christ, when we are born again in faith, our old lives die. Our new lives are totally with Christ. Our secret is our love for Him, which changes us. Love and faith combine to make us one with Him.

OUR STRENGTH

> Grace and peace to you from God our Father and
> the Lord Jesus Christ.
>
> —PHILIPPIANS 1:2

> And my God will meet all your needs according to
> his glorious riches in Christ Jesus.
>
> —PHILIPPIANS 4:19

All we need we are given from God. God gives us freedom from our sins through His grace, and peace from guilt and the troubles of this world. He will supply us all the power in the world as we need it. That gives us strength to live and believe confidently in Him

OUR MEDIATOR

> Therefore, since we have been justified through
> faith, we have peace with God through our Lord
> Jesus Christ.
>
> —ROMANS 5:1

We are brought into Christ, and He becomes our mediator, our lawyer and our counselor. Therefore, we have the peace of reconciliation, and we can enjoy peace with God through our Lord Jesus Christ, the Messiah. Christ is the Anointed One in whom we breathe and live. In our spiritual life we need nothing else. And when we place Christ as our highest priority in our spiritual life, everything else will be taken care of.

Prayer in Action

Chapter Three: Putting God First

For group discussion or personal reflection:

1. When do you act as a "branch" growing from the main vine—Jesus? When are you independent?

2. What are some specific ways you can make Jesus the foundation of your life?

3. Paul said he was ready to die for the Lord Jesus. What are some other examples of such faith in Jesus as our Lord? Do you have that much faith?

4. How do you show that you love Jesus? Do you model your life after Jesus' life? How?

5. How can you draw strength daily from knowing God will meet your needs?

6. Think about a time when you struggled with a problem. Did trusting and loving God help? How can it help in the future?

CHAPTER FOUR

PRAYER IN PRACTICE

*Do not be anxious about anything, but in everything, by prayer
and petition, with thanksgiving, present your requests to God.
And the peace of God, which transcends all understanding, will
guard your hearts and your minds in Christ Jesus.*

—PHILIPPIANS 4:6–7

Prayer determines how we prioritize God, people
and things in our lives. If we pray deeply and passionately, God is a higher priority than money,
careers or relationships with others. We put God above
and ahead of material things. Earlier, we talked about the
love relationship with God in the triangle of intimacy,
commitment and passion. That means we love our
Redeemer with all our heart and mind and soul and
strength. So, in our lifestyle of prayer, we are fervent,
faithful and focused because of that love.

The intimate communication of prayer with the Lord
gives us a feeling that God understands. It lets us know
that God is surrounding us with His presence, giving us
comfort and peace.

Yet one of the biggest problems we have is prayerless-
ness. People who are prayerless become overwhelmed,
broken down, pushed and defeated. We all have felt that
way when we've been out of prayer. It's a feeling we all
know and know well. And when our emotional gauge is
down and we feel alone and powerless, we set ourselves
up to sin.

So we must remember that God is able. Many people
post that reminder where they see it when they pray.
God can handle anything; all we need to do is turn everything over to Him. Prayer is the tool through which we're

29

in union with Him. It helps us keep in mind that God is always available to us.

But how do we practice prayer in our daily lives? Do we pray on a regular basis, or do we turn to God as a quick fix or last resort? Is our prayer merely a ritual, full of phrases made meaningless by repetition? Or have we filled our lives with prayer and been changed by an intimate relationship with our Lord?

Just as we would train for an athletic competition or prepare for our life's occupation, we must build our prayer life. Through the Scriptures, our Lord tells us how to align ourselves with Him in prayer. He gives us specific instructions to help us stay fervent, faithful and focused.

PRAY WITHOUT CEASING

> And pray in the Spirit on all occasions with all kinds of prayers and requests.
>
> —EPHESIANS 6:18

> Pray continually.
>
> —1 THESSALONIANS 5:17

The Scriptures are filled with reminders that we should always be in communication with God. We should surrender ourselves daily in prayer, in all our waking moments and at night. When we wake up at night, we should be thinking of our love for Him and not of the world and its anxieties. We should constantly be thinking of our Redeemer and of our relationship to Him as we go through our days. Staying in close contact with God helps us when the rough spots in our lives occur.

"I try to pray constantly—that is, every waking moment," says Dr. Ronald Haynes of Dunedin, Florida. He does this first because the Bible commands it and also because "my purpose in life is to please God—to be used for His purposes. The only way I know to do this is to place myself under the authority and power of Jesus Christ."

"I said 'I try' to pray constantly. And I do," Dr. Haynes says. "But I fall miserably short. But I'm spending more time in prayer now than I ever have in the past, and I know that I'll spend more time in the future than I do now.

"We can grow spiritually just as we grow intellectually and emotionally. By God's grace I have grown spiritually, and part of that growth involves spending more time communicating with God through prayer."

Author Richard J. Foster points out that we can pray any time, while at work, while driving in a car, while playing with our children, while making love. There is no wrong time. We just do it as we live. The seventeenth-century Puritan minister Richard Baxter said we also should make every time optimal for prayer. We should pray all the time, whether it is the right time or not, and then set aside times that are absolutely perfect for prayer.

In his book *Prayer*, Foster describes a spontaneous way to be in constant prayer with our Redeemer—breath prayers. These prayers are short and simple requests, spoken in one breath, asking God's help. They can be prayed continuously during the day, allowing us to keep our focus on our Redeemer. Foster says these prayers help him cope with whatever situations arise. And they remind us of God's grace in our daily lives.

Foster describes some of the prayers he uses to keep in touch with Jesus during the day. They can be a single word, such as "peace" or "faith," or a phrase such as "Teach me gentleness, Father." He suggests changing the prayer as a person moves through the week, to more specifically meet feelings or needs. For example, "Help me understand your truth, Lord" becomes "Help me live your truth, Lord," as we realize our needs.

The power of these simple prayers is further explained in Foster's book using the writings of mystic Frank Laubach. Laubach writes, "This sense of cooperation with God in little things is what so astonishes me, for I never have felt it this way before...my part is to live this hour in continuous inner conversation with God and in perfect responsiveness to His will. To make this hour gloriously rich. This seems to be all I need to think about."

PRAY WITH PERSISTENCE

Just as we pray continually, we should pray diligently. In Luke 18:2–8, Jesus tells a parable to show that we should always pray and not give up. It's the story of a woman who keeps pleading with a judge to grant her justice against an adversary. The judge, who neither feared God nor cared about men, refused for a while. But then he gave in to her request that justice be served because he realized she would wear him out with her pleas. Her persistence was rewarded.

In the same way, we know that God hears and answers our prayers when we cry out to Him and are aligned with Him. But we also know He is nothing like the judge. Where the judge is greedy and selfish, God is loving and compassionate—eager to hear from us and help us.

> And will not God bring about justice for his chosen ones, who cry out to him day and night? Will he keep putting them off? I tell you, he will see that they get justice, and quickly.
>
> —LUKE 18:6–8

BE SPECIFIC

Many of us pray in superficialities and generalities. Some people call this wholesale praying. We pray, "I love you, Lord. Thank you for all the things, forgive all my sins, bless everybody and give me all I need." But when we are specific, our hearts are turned to God in faith. If we are vague in our prayers, we don't truly hand our lives over to God. We don't give Him enough credit to take care of us. It's only when we get down to brass tacks that we surrender ourselves to Him and seek His will. We then pray about specific problems and praise Him for specific blessings.

But we must be careful when we pray for specific solutions. We also need to pray that God's will be done. Our prayers cannot be marching orders for God to carry out, or a wish list of things we might desire for a moment or two. When our hearts are inclined to Him, our requests are in line with His will.

Write It Down

Use a journal to keep track of how you are growing closer to God. Write down all your spiritual requests as well as requests you make as an intercessor for others and anything else you seek of Him. Write out the Scriptures you are reading and what the Lord and Holy Spirit are telling you those Scriptures are saying to you.

Then go back and review what happened with those requests or petitions and how the Scriptures applied to specific circumstances or problems.

Journals help us see God's hand at work daily in our lives and, when times are tough, remind us of His faithfulness and love. We are reminded that God is able, and we never have to go it alone.

Be in Union With God

Do we actually pray because of tradition, not because we really feel the need to or want to? We must do more than just call God's name in our prayers, in our work, in our relationships. We must be in communion with Him, making His will for our lives our top priority.

The Old Testament story of the Israelites fighting the Philistines shows us the importance of believing the Lord is with us. In one battle with the Philistines, the Israelites lost four thousand men. So they decided to carry the Ark of the Covenant into the next battle with them, using it as a banner. Yet they were not surrendered to God when they carried the ark. They put on the title of God without putting Him in their hearts. And in the second battle, thirty thousand people were killed and the ark was captured.

In the same way, if we put on the label of God and charge foolishly rather than having Him in our hearts and making Him part of us, we fail. But when God becomes part of our lives, we overcome.

Jews in Jesus' day said there were 611 different commandments—365 were negative, 246 were positive. We can have that many regarding our prayer life, making it a ritual rather than a relationship. Jesus gives us an enriched image of God, telling us to first love Him and then love others as ourselves. It is through that love that prayer becomes a relationship. Without that love, our prayers are empty words.

PRAY HUMBLY

> And when you pray, do not be like the hypocrites, for they love to pray standing in the synagogues and on the street corners to be seen by men. I tell you the truth, they have their reward in full. But when you pray, go into your room, close the door and pray to your Father, who is unseen. Then your Father, who sees what is done in secret, will reward you. And when you pray, do not keep on babbling like pagans, for they think they will be heard because of their many words. Do not be like them, for your Father knows what you need before you ask him.
>
> —MATTHEW 6:5–8

Jesus gives us some specific guidelines to help us pray humbly and honestly. These guidelines show us that the manner in which we pray reflects the attitude in which we come to God. It's difficult to pray humbly to God if we're worried about appearances. When we pray using these guidelines, we're focused on the substance of our

relationship with our Lord, and we don't worry about
trying to impress God or others with our style.
It is our humility that realizes the great gap between
God and us and is thankful for His saving grace. We
realize that we need His grace and guidance, that we can
do nothing on our own. And as we humble ourselves
before God, we begin to see His greatness more and more.

> O LORD, our Lord,
>   how majestic is your name in all the earth!
> You have set your glory
>   above the heavens.
> From the lips of children and infants
>   you have ordained praise
> because of your enemies,
>   to silence the foe and the avenger.
> When I consider your heavens,
>   the work of your fingers,
> the moon and the stars,
>   which you have set in place,
> what is man that you are mindful of him,
>   the son of man that you care for him?
> You made him a little lower than the heavenly
>   beings
>   and crowned him with glory and honor.
> You made him ruler over the works of your hands;
>   you put everything under his feet:
> all flocks and herds,
>   and the beasts of the field,
> the birds of the air,
>   and the fish of the sea,
>   all that swim the paths of the seas.
> O LORD, our Lord,
>   how majestic is your name in all the earth!
>   —PSALM 8

One of the greatest roadblocks to praying is our desire
to be independent. This breeds pride, conceit, cynicism
and arrogance, just to name a few. We want to be scientific,

to be self-sufficient. We don't want to admit we are not in complete control.

When we have this attitude, prayer is difficult. It interferes with our ambitions and desires. We must give up the desire for those things that normally motivate us—money, admiration from our peers, independence—to see God more clearly and to be open to His guidance. Jesus shows us how we must humble ourselves before our Creator.

> Your attitude should be the same as that of Christ Jesus: Who, being in very nature God, did not consider equality with God something to be grasped, but made himself nothing, taking the very nature of a servant, being made in human likeness. And being found in appearance as a man, he humbled himself and became obedient to death—even death on a cross!
>
> —PHILIPPIANS 2:5–8

When we relinquish our desire for control, we can feel more fully His Holy Spirit upon us, and we can feel His firm fingers of control guiding our hands in whatever we do.

I strive to align myself with the Lord through the Holy Spirit as I work and as I encounter people throughout my day. I know that I have to give up self-centered independence and submit myself, through prayer, to be in a relationship with the Lord and my patients. Psalm 147:6 reassures me: "The Lord sustains the humble but casts the wicked to the ground."

PRAY WITH FAITH

> Therefore I tell you, whatever you ask for in prayer, believe that you have received it, and it will be yours.
>
> —MARK 11:24

We pray humbly, recognizing God's greatness and our dependence on Him. But as we pray we believe He loves us and hears our prayers. His greatness doesn't keep Him from us. His greatness is what makes Him our Redeemer and Provider. We pray full of faith that we have received what we ask for from the One who is our Light and Salvation.

Indeed, there is no real praying to God for ourselves or for others until faith is born in the heart. Jesus tells us that when we pray, we must believe that we have received. We shouldn't sit around wondering. Through our faithfulness and obedience we show our Redeemer how much we love and trust Him. And we know He will provide for us.

> If any of you lacks wisdom, he should ask God, who gives generously to all without finding fault, and it will be given to him. But when he asks, he must believe and not doubt, because he who doubts is like a wave of the sea, blown and tossed by the wind. That man should not think he will receive anything from the Lord; he is a double-minded man, unstable in all he does.
>
> —JAMES 1:5–8

Faith builds upon faith. As we believe in God and see evidence of His work, we believe more and have more faith in His power. We also respond with more passion for studying His Word and a greater dependence on the Holy Spirit.

Soon after his Christian conversion, Tampa cardiologist Dr. Peter Knight witnessed God miraculously heal one of his patients from a disease considered hopeless and terminal. Dr. Knight prayed only for God's will to be done. "I don't ask questions or analyze now," Dr. Knight said. "I just listen to the Holy Spirit and obey. As I do so, I find my faith to believe for the miracles increasing. Faith builds upon our maturity to stand on His Word and to do what it says."

How we implement our faith is very important, too. I

have a friend who knows the Word, teaches the Word and is enthusiastic. Yet she is anxious and doesn't sleep well at night. She talks about trusting the Lord, but she can't rest in the Lord. We have to trust before we can realize the peace of God.

There's a story about a mountain climber who was falling from a high point. As he fell, he grabbed a limb and was holding on for dear life. He suddenly became very religious, and he yelled up to heaven, "Is anybody up there? Pleeease help me!" He yelled this three or four times. Finally a deep, deep voice said, "Yes, I'm here. Let go, and I'll take care of you." The mountain climber thought about this for a few minutes as he hung on to the branch and then he yelled, "Is there anybody else up there?"

We are like that mountain climber. We want to know whether there's anyone up there to fill our emptiness and our loneliness. We want to know whether anyone hears our cries. But we don't want someone who will require that we totally let go. We still want to be in control. Therefore, faith is critical for us to be able to let go and let God. Second Corinthians 5:7 tells us to "live by faith, not by sight."

SPEAK THE WORD OF GOD AND BE FILLED WITH THE HOLY SPIRIT

> Then you will call upon me and come and pray to me, and I will listen to you. You will seek me and find me when you seek me with all your heart.
>
> —JEREMIAH 29:12–13

Meditating on God's Word is a key way to align our hearts with God before we approach Him in prayer. That time of meditation can help prepare our hearts for hearing God's voice and being focused solely on Him. That attitude is what the Lord wants of us. Hosea 6:6 says, "For I desire mercy, not sacrifice, and acknowledgment of God rather than burnt offerings."

God also commands us to learn His Word and speak it in prayer to receive His blessings. Unless we are able to pray the Word of God, our prayers are not proper. We must push out the world and its distractions and push in the Word of God before we can pray adequately alone with God or with others. Then we are able to pray with the great expectation of His power being demonstrated in, through and for us.

But mouthing words or putting on the appearance of holiness with no inner transformation by the Holy Spirit gets us nowhere. Not until we have been born of the Holy Spirit can we truly pray spiritual prayers. Our prayers can't be spiritual until we have the Holy Spirit living within us. Romans 8:9 says, "You, however, are controlled not by the sinful nature but by the Spirit, if the Spirit of God lives in you. And if anyone does not have the Spirit of Christ, he does not belong to Christ."

The Reverend Jack Taylor says that frequently we're full of the Holy Spirit but not based in the Word. Or we may be full of the Word but not filled with the Holy Spirit. We need the Word and the Holy Spirit to come together in our lives and in our prayers. Only then do our prayers have power and our lives have true meaning.

The Word alone is dead. It must be anointed in us by the Holy Spirit. The Holy Spirit must work with the Word to be full in our lives. Otherwise we may be driven by emotions, not the Spirit. We must be full of the Holy Spirit as we are full of the Word. They are not separated. A focus solely on the Spirit without the Word can turn to emotionalism. A focus on the Word without the Spirit can turn to formalism.

Let me give you an example of the need for these two elements to work together: There was a preacher who had no preparation; he just asked for a miracle when he stood in the pulpit each Sunday. Another preacher studied for hours but didn't ask for God's help. Each of them was inadequately prepared. One wanted a miracle as he stood in the pulpit and asked the Holy Spirit to come upon him. The second preacher came with thirty hours of preparation, but he was totally independent. He had studied intellectually but did not ask for the Holy Spirit's guidance. Both would be inadequate. Until the two can come together—asking God's miracle through the Holy Spirit and preparing oneself in the Word—a fine sermon will not come forth.

It is the same way with prayer. When we are filled with the Word and the Holy Spirit, prayer changes us and changes the world.

THE WILL TO PRAY, THE DESIRE TO PRAY

Do we pray because we will ourselves to do it, or because we desire communion with our Lord? Just as the love relationship between a man and woman needs to be based not on will but on the desire to become close to one another, so must the relationship with God.

Married couples have become married. First they know each other, then care for and become familiar with each other and then commit themselves to each other. That's how our relationship with God grows. First we know Him, then care for Him, become familiar with Him and totally commit ourselves to Him. Through that, our love for Him grows and becomes richer.

If we pray by will alone, we don't have a full relationship with God. We can will ourselves to go to church, read His Word and pray, but unless our hearts are inclined to God and we love Him, we don't accomplish much. When we will ourselves to do it, we depend on our own strength, and then we dry up and become discouraged. It requires greater effort, and we get tired and want to give up.

It is because we love our Lord that we worship Him, read His Word and pray. These actions come from the deep passion we feel when our hearts are inclined to God. And when we're abiding in the Holy Spirit, our lives are changed, and we desire to do His work and His will.

For example, I may pray daily with my wife. We may do it because we will to do it, so it may have no significance or meaning. However, if our hearts are inclined toward God and each other, we become closer to the Lord and together grow closer to Him. We do it out of a deeper sense of the Holy Spirit acting in us.

So before we can truly pray, our hearts must be inclined to God. Then we will develop the will and incorporate it into our lives. The Holy Spirit's prompting results in actions.

Praying in Tongues

Some people pray in tongues as a way of aligning themselves with Christ. Just as some people pray on their knees or some pray standing, some use prayer in tongues as another method to be in contact with Christ.

If they are sincere in their hearts and are seeking the Lord's presence, it is a way to keep close to the Lord. People who use this technique find that it works many times when there seems to be dryness in the spirit.

In Conclusion

Prayer unites us with our Redeemer. Through prayer we know God's heart and His will, and we align ourselves with Him. We seek God because we love Him and want to be in communion with Him. So, increasingly, we want His presence in our daily lives. We pray unceasingly, turning our lives over to Him and putting Him in charge of all the problems, as well as rejoicing in all the gifts He gives. And when we pray, we know He hears and responds to us as His children. In that growing relationship of love we long for God as more than our friend. He is our Creator and Redeemer, and we find peace in Him.

As the deer pants for streams of water, so my soul pants for you, O God.

—PSALM 42:1

PRAYER IN ACTION

CHAPTER FOUR: PRAYER IN PRACTICE

For group discussion or personal reflection:

1. When have you been "out of prayer"—feeling too overwhelmed or defeated to pray? How did you feel? What helped you start praying again?

2. What are some "breath prayers" you could pray? What other ways could you pray without ceasing?

3. Think about a time when you were especially close to God in prayer. What happened to bring that closeness about? Are you still that close?

4. What are the roadblocks to being humble in your prayer life?

5. Think about a time when God has answered your prayer. When you prayed, did you believe the prayer was already answered? How difficult is it to pray with such faith all the time?

6. It's important to be grounded in God's Word and also abide in the Holy Spirit. Do these work together in your life?

7. Couples become married. How can you adapt that process to your prayer relationship with God?

CHAPTER FIVE

A BALANCED APPROACH

*Do not be anxious about anything, but in everything, by
prayer and petition, with thanksgiving, present your
requests to God.*

—PHILIPPIANS 4:6

Our prayers to our Redeemer must be balanced. When we exercise, it's important to strengthen all our muscles, not just our arms or legs. In the same way, we should balance our communion with God. For example, we cannot go to Him only with requests. We must have balanced prayer for the different parts of our lives.

One mnemonic to use in remembering the different elements of prayer is ACTS: Adoration, Confession, Thanksgiving and Supplication.

ADORATION

Praise the LORD, O my soul, and forget not all his
benefits.

—PSALM 103:2

Our adoration of God is our greatest joy. That joy should permeate our work and our relationships with our spouse, family and others—our entire life for our entire lifetime. For God is our Redeemer, not only our friend. He is the Creator of the universe and is sovereign over all things. How can we do less than adore Him? The adoration and worship of God should be where we find the greatest fulfillment, joy and delight in being a person.

French theologian and religious reformer John Calvin said we can never thank God enough for His grace and His salvation, but we can praise Him for it. We can never equal His grace, but we can just simply thank Him for it in our praise and thanksgiving.

The Psalms are full of prayers of praise and rejoicing in the Lord. Contemplating on the Psalms can help put us in the posture of praise. In my own life, praising the Lord and affirming His works fills me with hope, and it gives me the grace to move beyond the concerns of this world.

CONFESSION

> If we claim to be without sin, we deceive our-
> selves and the truth is not in us. If we confess our
> sins, he is faithful and just and will forgive us our
> sins and purify us from all unrighteousness. If we
> claim we have not sinned, we make him out to be
> a liar and his word has no place in our lives.
>
> —1 JOHN 1:8–10

Satan is at work daily to separate us from God by sin. He has many tools at his disposal, but perhaps his greatest are our own lack of faith in God and our desire to be independent. The Bible is full of stories of those who have fallen short. They failed to put their trust in God, relying instead on their own abilities. Time and time again, the minute we turn from God, we fail, and we sin against Him.

But God's Word also gives us God's promise—that He will stay with us and continue loving us even when, especially when, we fail. He knows we are sinful beings. That's why He sent His son—to die that we might live.

Our Creator and Redeemer knows everything about us. He knows our most obvious strengths and weaknesses and our innermost secrets. We don't have to confess our sins so that He knows about them. He already knows. Instead, confession allows us to face up to our wrongs, to admit them and seek God's help in conquering them. Sin breaks the communion we have with God. Confession restores it.

> Then I acknowledged my sin to you and did not
> cover up my iniquity. I said, "I will confess my
> transgressions to the LORD"—and you forgave the
> guilt of my sin.
>
> —PSALM 32:5

Therefore, we should be specific in confessing all our
sin. That goes beyond a list of all the wrongs we've committed. It also includes the sins of omission, the times we
should have acted but didn't. As James 4:17 says,
"Anyone, then, who knows the good he ought to do and
doesn't do it, sins." We also must confess our times of
unbelief in our Lord. Martin Luther said we need a daily
repentance, possibly constant repentance, asking for the
Lord to be merciful.

That's a tall order, and one that could make us want to
give up if we feel overwhelmed or think it's too much for
God to forgive. But we have His assurance that He will
forgive us. Psalm 103:12 says, "As far as the east is from
the west, so far has he removed our transgressions from
us."

THANKSGIVING

> You are my God, and I will give you thanks; you
> are my God, and I will exalt you. Give thanks to
> the LORD, for he is good; his love endures forever.
>
> —PSALM 118:28–29

> Give thanks in all circumstances, for this is God's
> will for you in Christ Jesus.
>
> —1 THESSALONIANS 5:18

Prayer should change us by our thanksgiving, by our
rejoicing in our Creator. We should want to give thanks
for all that God has provided us and all the difficult times
we face. I thank the Lord each day for my patients, for
the ones who are healed and the ones who are not. I
thank Him for my family, my friends and my practice. I

thank Him for the bad days as well as the good.

When we're in an attitude of thanksgiving, we acknowledge God as our Redeemer and we align ourselves with Him. Thanking the Lord for the good and the not-so-good aspects of our lives and rejoicing in Him can lift us above the drudgery and difficulty of whatever crosses we are carrying. Practicing that attitude of thanksgiving leads us to contentment in God, not indifference. We know that God is in control, and we find peace in that.

SUPPLICATION

> Then they cried to the LORD in their trouble, and he saved them from their distress.
>
> —PSALM 107:13

The dictionary defines supplication as "a humble request, prayer, petition." We know God wants us to seek Him in times of trouble. He wants us to turn to Him, to rely on His strength rather than our own. In the same way, we should seek God's help for others.

"My intercessory prayer for my patients begins the moment I awaken," says Dr. James A. Avery of Clearwater, Florida. "I usually start the day (with my head still on the pillow) asking the Lord to guide me, give me wisdom and insight, and help me to be a light for Him during the upcoming day. I will often pray for specific patients who are in the hospital or especially ill."

AN EVOLVING PRAYER LIFE

Dr. William Hale of Clearwater, Florida describes an evolution in the elements of prayer. The first kind of prayer we offer, he says, is as a child. It is perhaps the purest prayer because it is made on faith alone. We have no experience with evil, no hurts, no disappointments, no losses, no injuries, no deceptions, no betrayals and no denials. "Here I am; I may be walking through the valley of the shadow of death, but I am not afraid. I place myself in your hands; watch over me, care for me and protect me, for I love you. I have faith in you and I know you love me. Because I do, I am going to be all right."

The second kind of prayer takes place much later, he says. When we have had several life-threatening events, our prayer relates to the vicissitudes of life and asks for forgiveness for being unkind and for our lack of faith.

Then we move to the third kind of prayer—prayer for someone and something. Prayer for someone, for example, could be for a person in a threatening situation that presents the chance for self-determination. Prayer for something may include seeking reform of some societal issues. These types of prayers provide "comfort and reassurance, peace and contentment," Dr. Hale says.

Finally, there is the prayer of thanksgiving. "Thanks is not just for the time when we have recovered from an illness or accident," Dr. Hale says. "Thanksgiving is for all times; prayer is for all times."

"I guess my struggle for maturation in my religious beliefs has allowed me to see this more than ever before," Dr. Hale says. "Prayer [for others] has been with them when they are happy and for them when they are sad. It has been with them when they have sought relief and for them as they have entered the final transition, for 'If you believe, you will receive whatever you ask for in prayer'" (Matthew 21:22).

PRAYER IN ACTION

CHAPTER FIVE: A BALANCED APPROACH

For group discussion or personal reflection:

1. How can prayer help you praise God throughout every day?

2. How easy is it to confess your sins to God? Is it difficult to believe that once they're confessed, God forgives them?

3. Can you really thank God for the bad days as well as the good?

4. Is it as easy to pray for others as it is for yourself?

5. Are your prayers balanced? Which element of prayer is the most difficult for you? Which is the easiest?

6. It's easy to ask God's help in times of trouble. How can this balanced approach help you build a regular prayer time and a stronger prayer life?

7. Using Dr. Hale's model, how far has your prayer life matured?

PART TWO

HEARTS INCLINED TO GOD

CHAPTER SIX

ROADBLOCKS TO PRAYER

P rayer is the way to grow closer to our Creator and to align ourselves with His will. Yet no matter how much we desire that relationship and want to show our love for Him, we're never free from obstacles. We must battle our own egos, the agendas of our families and peers, and what the world tells us about success to stay in a relationship of prayer with our Lord.

When we are aligned with God, our priorities are in line with His will, and we feel loved and protected. When we get away from God, we can start to feel sorry for ourselves when times get rough. We begin to believe we aren't getting the love or recognition we deserve.

When we align ourselves with the pull of worldly influences, we are no longer controlled by the Lord. We find ourselves being selfish, covetous, proud and uncaring. Then we become irrational and start making bad decisions based on worry or fear. We worry that we're not getting ahead quickly enough in our careers or in the accumulation of worldly possessions. We're afraid of what others might say or think of us. We buy into the world's view of success and join the "rat race." We base our decisions and actions on pleasing others. James 3:16 says, "For where you have envy and selfish ambition, there you find disorder and every evil practice."

How does all this happen? Can it happen if we're in communion with God? No matter how strong our spirit is, as long as we're housed in earthly temples, we'll always struggle to overcome the weaknesses of the flesh. We will struggle against our egos, the demands of our jobs and families, and the temptations Satan puts in our path.

The humility that is so necessary for our salvation is

so often gone. The humility that is so necessary for our being filled with the Holy Spirit is so often not present. There is no way we can be filled with the Holy Spirit and the Word and pray passionately and deeply until we have emptied ourselves of pride and the things that go along with it, such as the desire for wealth and power.

To keep us from succumbing to the subtle temptations that pull us away from God, we must deny ourselves, take up our cross and follow the Lord with all our heart. That may sound easier said than done. But God has given us an example of submitting to His will in the life and death of his Son, Jesus. With every fiber of His being crying for life, Jesus submitted to His father's will and died so that we might live.

Prayer is a key to staying faithful and following His example. Watchful prayer helps us be victorious over those temptations, because during that time with our Lord we receive the guidance and direction that keep us focused on God's will. Then we base our decisions on His will, not our own. And our mind, body and behavior will be inclined to Him in everything we do.

The battle against worldly influences that keep us from a life of prayer is never over. Let's look at some of the pitfalls to prayer and how we can identify them and fight back.

LACK OF FAITH

> Without faith, it is impossible to please God, because anyone who comes to him must believe that he exists and that he rewards those who earnestly seek him.
>
> —HEBREWS 11:6

Faith avoids the burnout and anxieties that occur as we live and struggle in this competitive world. Faith is our response to Christ. We must live a life of faith knowing that the Lord provides and takes care of us. His grace is sufficient for everything.

Yet there are still times when we doubt God and His Word. We can be limited in our relationship of prayer when we don't see the expanse of God. We can fail to look at Him with all our heart and, in our whole being, have faith in Him. Even the disciples, who lived and walked with Jesus and saw Him perform many miracles, doubted Him.

> During the fourth watch of the night Jesus went out to them, walking on the lake. When the disciples saw him walking on the lake, they were terrified. "It's a ghost," they said, and cried out in fear.
>
> But Jesus immediately said to them: "Take courage! It is I. Don't be afraid." "Lord, if it's you," Peter replied, "tell me to come to you on the water." "Come," he said.
>
> Then Peter got down out of the boat, walked on the water and came toward Jesus. But when he saw the wind, he was afraid and, beginning to sink, cried out, "Lord, save me!" Immediately Jesus reached out his hand and caught him. "You of little faith," he said, "why did you doubt?"
>
> —MATTHEW 14:25–31

We can be the same way, walking along in faith until we see the storm around us. Then we get scared and want to take charge. We begin to sink in our troubles because we have taken our eyes off our Lord.

God knows it requires faith to believe in Him and put total trust and total control of our lives in His hands. Faith comes by hearing the Word of God. It is our response to hearing that Word and using it in our lives. He also reassures us of the blessings we receive when we do hand Him the reins. Jesus tells the disciples in John 20:29, "Because you have seen me, you have believed; blessed are those who have not seen and yet have believed."

Our faith needs to be so strong that it doesn't allow the cares of the world to interfere with our lifestyle of prayer. As our faith grows, so grows our ability to let God be in charge, to remember that He is in control and to surrender ourselves to Him. We pray with confidence that He hears our prayers and will provide for us.

Yet when we pray with faith, we must be sure we aren't giving God directions. Faith can give way to pride, and we begin to tell God what to do, rather than seeking His will. There are two parts of a person—the controlling side and the caring or nurturing side. Prayer to our Redeemer must bring both parts together so we pray with an attitude of faith, not arrogance. If faith doesn't represent our relationship with God, then our relationship is superficial.

PRIDE AND SELFISHNESS

> And what does the LORD require of you? To act justly and to love mercy and to walk humbly with your God.
>
> —MICAH 6:8

Pride is one of the biggest roadblocks to prayer. When we begin to think we can do things ourselves, when we want to be independent and put ourselves first, we don't live a lifestyle of surrender to our Lord. And when we think we can handle things ourselves, we begin to stop relying on God and seeking Him in prayer.

Lucifer gives us the most powerful example of what can happen when pride overtakes us.

> You were anointed as a guardian cherub, for so I ordained you. You were on the holy mount of God; you walked among the fiery stones. You were blameless in your ways from the day you were created till wickedness was found in you.
>
> —EZEKIEL 28:14–15

Lucifer walked closest to the throne of the Almighty

until he became prideful and wanted to take God's place. This pride led to Lucifer's rebellion against God and to his ruin.

> How you have fallen from heaven, O morning star, son of the dawn! You have been cast down to the earth, you who once laid low the nations! You said in your heart, "I will ascend to heaven; I will raise my throne above the stars of God; I will sit enthroned on the mount of assembly, on the utmost heights of the sacred mountain. I will ascend above the tops of the clouds; I will make myself like the Most High."
>
> —ISAIAH 14:12–14

Closely associated with pride is the independence Lucifer showed when he said, "I will do this," and "I will do that." An independent spirit will not long be tolerated in the presence of God. Wanting to rely on our own skills and abilities to succeed adds up to sin. We leave our attitudes of independence and pride behind when we realize we can't live without prayer.

As teenagers, we all wanted to be grown up and out on our own in the world—independent from our families and God, making our own way and making our own decisions. We battle the same attitude in our relationship with our Father. But this is the opposite of what Jesus tells us. Being independent separates us from the Lord and His power. Jesus says:

> I am the vine; you are the branches. If a man remains in me and I in him, he will bear much fruit; apart from me you can do nothing. If anyone does not remain in me, he is like a branch that is thrown away and withers; such branches are picked up, thrown into the fire and burned. If you remain in me and my words remain in you, ask whatever you wish, and it will be given you.
>
> —JOHN 15:5–7

Our dependence on Him increases as we commune with our Lord more in prayer. Then His will becomes our will. His desires become our desires. His standard of success becomes ours.

The only coping mechanism I have when I am overwhelmed by the daily battle is to relax in the Lord instead of trying to fix everything myself. Proverbs tells us that pride comes before a fall. That is as true in medicine as in any facet of life. An important part of being a good doctor is being humble first. It is essential to be humble, dependent and totally filled with the Holy Spirit before I can share the healing power that comes from God.

Frequently when we are disappointed with ourselves, we project that disappointment to others. That disappointment leads to anger and the anger to depression. We lash out against what we now perceive as the problem—the other person. We feel betrayed when we betray. We project our unfaithfulness, our sins, and all our problems on others rather than trying to clear them up and restore our inner peace.

We can do the same thing to God. We can blame Him for our disappointments, for feeling betrayed, for being unfaithful, when the blame really falls on our shoulders.

Through prayer we can keep our desires aligned with God's will for our lives. When we are in communion with Him, our hearts are inclined to His, and we trust that He will take care of us. We no longer need to worry about providing for ourselves. He will provide.

Once we put our faith in Him, we realize how dependent we are. Our own efforts pale in comparison with the power of the Almighty, and we're humble in His presence. We're happy serving the Lord, and He will bless us. Jesus tells us in Luke 14:11, "For everyone who exalts himself will be humbled, and he who humbles himself will be exalted."

IMPATIENCE

> I waited patiently for the LORD; he turned to me
> and heard my cry.
>
> —PSALM 40:1

We know God answers prayers, but there are times we want Him to follow our own timetable and not His. When we're impatient, we begin to lose faith that He will answer us or will not give us what we want, so we try to take matters into our own hands. We battle God for control of our lives. Instead, we need to have faith that He will provide for us because He loves us, but for His glory and not our own.

In John 11, we're given an example of Jesus using His own timetable. Two sisters, Mary and Martha, sent a message to Jesus, asking Him to come to their village to heal their brother Lazarus, who was sick. John 11:4–6 says:

> When he heard this, Jesus said, "This sickness will not end in death. No, it is for God's glory so that God's Son may be glorified through it."
> Jesus loved Martha and her sister and Lazarus. Yet when he heard that Lazarus was sick, he stayed where he was two more days.

Then Jesus and his disciples went to Bethany. But He knew that Lazarus was already dead. And by the time they got to Bethany, Lazarus had been dead four days.

> "Lord," Martha said to Jesus, "if you had been here, my brother would not have died. But I know that even now God will give you whatever you ask."
>
> —JOHN 11:21–22

Jesus then raised Lazarus from the dead. Rather than rushing to Bethany, as Mary and Martha wanted, Jesus operated in His own time frame, using Lazarus' death and resurrection to prove His power so others would believe in Him.

Failure to wait on God greatly hinders our relationship with Him. And impatience, in direct opposition to God's commands, may even lead to more sin.

Saul, the king of Israel, grew impatient while waiting for the return of the prophet Samuel. The Lord had anointed Samuel as a priest whose duties included leading the sacrificial worship before Saul's armies left for war. Saul decided he couldn't wait any longer before one battle. He overstepped his bounds and decided to perform the ceremony himself. This impatience had far-reaching consequences:

> Saul remained at Gilgal, and all the troops with him were quaking with fear. He waited seven days, the time set by Samuel; but Samuel did not come to Gilgal, and Saul's men began to scatter. So he said, "Bring me the burnt offering and the fellowship offerings." And Saul offered up the burnt offering. Just as he finished making the offering, Samuel arrived, and Saul went out to greet him. "What have you done?" asked Samuel. Saul replied, "When I saw that the men were scattering and that you did not come at the set time...I felt compelled to offer the burnt offering." "You acted foolishly," Samuel said. "You have not kept the command the LORD your God gave you; if you had, he would have established your kingdom over Israel for all time. But now your kingdom will not endure; the LORD has sought out a man after his own heart and appointed him leader of his people, because you have not kept the LORD's command."
>
> —1 SAMUEL 13:7–14

Saul's fear of losing in battle was greater than his faith in the Lord. Rather than turning to God in prayer and giving God control of the situation, Saul took matters into his own hands. His failure to wait upon God's prophet proved disastrous to his relationship with God and to his future.

Saul didn't want to wait on God. Martha knew that even though it seemed too late to save her brother, Jesus was in control. Psalm 27:14 gives us confidence when we get impatient: "Wait for the Lord; be strong and take heart and wait for the Lord." Having confidence and faith that God will provide can get us through many situations in which we want to turn from God and turn to our own solutions.

LAZINESS

Prayer is active, not passive. Even when we meditate quietly, seeking God's voice, we are faithful, fervent and focused on Him. Building a lifestyle of prayer requires earnest commitment and hard work.

The spiritually lazy person is not prepared to enter the presence of God. He cannot be inclined to God if he doesn't spend the time and energy in prayer to know God's heart. But those who pray eagerly and earnestly look forward to being united with the Lord. Prayer is a joy, and communion with God is something we desire and seek with anticipation.

A prayerful life requires much effort and sacrifice. It requires us to develop ourselves physically and mentally—training that can be similar to training for an athletic competition or an academic endeavor. We must commit to spending the time and energy needed to build a lifestyle of prayer. And we must do it because we love our Lord, not because we will it to happen.

If we consider prayer just a duty rather than a passionate response to God, laziness and indifference can result. In a marriage in which one or both partners consider the relationship an obligation or duty, the fires of love grow cold. The same can happen with our Lord if we do not actively and passionately seek His presence in our lives.

No Time to Pray

Do you find yourself doing more and praying less? We might be seeking significance through our own works. We may be so busy being responsible that it interferes with our ability to listen and grow through prayer. Jesus' words to Mary and Martha give us a hint about the busyness that keeps us from growing closer to our Lord:

> She had a sister called Mary, who sat at the Lord's feet listening to what he said. But Martha was distracted by all the preparations that had to be made. She came to him and asked, "Lord, don't you care that my sister has left me to do the work by myself? Tell her to help me!"
>
> "Martha, Martha," the Lord answered, "you are worried and upset about many things, but only one thing is needed. Mary has chosen what is better, and it will not be taken away from her."
>
> —LUKE 10:39–42

Martha wanted to rely on her own efforts, not trusting that all those tasks would be accomplished. But Mary chose to spend time looking to Jesus and loving Him. She made Jesus her priority and set aside other tasks and responsibilities to be with Him. Which one more accurately describes you?

A Critical Spirit

The habit of finding fault with everything and everyone destroys our humble communion with God in prayer. Jesus set the example for us by seeking to deliver us from our sinful ways rather than simply condemning us. John 3:17 says, "For God did not send his Son into the world to condemn the world, but to save the world through him."

When we criticize rather than encourage and correct, we condemn not only those we criticize but also ourselves. The Scriptures are clear on this point:

You, therefore, have no excuse, you who pass judgment on someone else, for at whatever point you judge the other, you are condemning yourself, because you who pass judgment do the same things.

—ROMANS 2:1

Do not judge, or you too will be judged. For in the same way you judge others, you will be judged, and with the measure you use, it will be measured to you.

—MATTHEW 7:1–2

Don't grumble against each other, brothers, or you will be judged.

—JAMES 5:9

A critical or judgmental spirit takes our attention away from the perfection of God; we're focused instead on the imperfections of others. We cannot pray with our whole being if we let ourselves be distracted by critical thoughts about others. And as long as we're pointing out another's weaknesses, we don't have time in prayer to seek God's forgiveness and allow Him to cleanse us from our own sin.

For if you forgive men when they sin against you, your heavenly Father will also forgive you. But if you do not forgive men their sins, your Father will not forgive your sins.

—MATTHEW 6:14–15

HYPOCRISY

A life formed by prayer is a life opposed to illusion, self-deception and hypocrisy...prayer is at war with falsehood.

—THEODORE W. JENNINGS, *LIFE AS WORSHIP*

Our attitudes play a premier role in our ability to pray. Time after time in the Scriptures, we find our Lord confronting the pious appearances of religious leaders. In the Book of Matthew, He told them in no uncertain terms:

> Woe to you, teachers of the law and Pharisees, you hypocrites! You clean the outside of the cup and dish, but inside they are full of greed and self-indulgence. Blind Pharisee! First clean the inside of the cup and dish, and then the outside also will be clean. Woe to you, teachers of the law and Pharisees, you hypocrites! You are like white-washed tombs, which look beautiful on the outside but on the inside are full of dead men's bones and everything unclean. In the same way, on the outside you appear to people as righteous but on the inside you are full of hypocrisy and wickedness.
>
> —MATTHEW 23:25–28

Jesus spoke for the Father. He wants hearts of loving obedience, not showy outward displays. His rebuke serves only to reemphasize the Lord's concern about our inner disposition. Though we may not consider ourselves as hypocritical as the Pharisees, we who have become "living temples of the Holy Spirit" still need regular cleaning.

> Create in me a pure heart, O God, and renew a steadfast spirit within me.
>
> —PSALM 51:10

Just as Jesus drove out the unclean activities from the earthly temple in Jerusalem, so He purges us. When we seek Him with our whole heart, we come to Him ready to submit ourselves to Him. In a lifestyle of prayer, we continually confess where we have fallen short in our faith and in our actions, and we seek His grace. In our weakness before our Redeemer, we find His strength. When we admit our faults, we see His perfection.

Worldly Influences

> Do not love the world or anything in the world. If anyone loves the world, the love of the Father is not in him. For everything in the world—the craving of sinful man, the lust of his eyes and the boasting of what he has and does—comes not from the Father but from the world. The world and its desires pass away, but the man who does the will of God lives forever.
>
> —1 John 2:15–17

We can never have a close relationship with our Lord in prayer if we have affection for the things of this world. The reason is simple: no person can serve two masters. He will love one and hate the other. We may need to take a close look at our priorities and bring them back into focus so we can be faithful and fervent in our prayers. If we worship anything other than God, our prayers are not honest communion with our Lord.

Once we have been born again in the Spirit of the Lord, we no longer belong to this world. We become strangers passing through a foreign land on the way to an eternal, heavenly kingdom. When we know this, we'll find it easier to say no to the world's attractions.

It also helps to recognize who hides behind the scenes trying to steal what rightfully belongs to God. Satan wants to replace God as the lord of our heart and make us bow in obedience to him. The devil even tempted Jesus at the beginning of His earthly ministry:

> Again, the devil took him to a very high mountain and showed him all the kingdoms of the world and their splendor. "All this I will give you," he said, "if you will bow down and worship me."
>
> —Matthew 4:8–9

Jesus resisted Satan's temptations by relying on the Word of God.

> Jesus said to him, "Away from me, Satan! For it is written, 'Worship the Lord your God, and serve him only.'"
>
> —MATTHEW 4:10

In the same way, we must rely on the Holy Spirit and the Word to resist the pull of worldly desires. When we are focused on God and His promises, we find the strength to fend off temptations. Psalm 32:7 says, "You are my hiding place; you will protect me from trouble and surround me with songs of deliverance."

Yet the influence of this world can creep into our lives if we're not diligent in our prayers. For it is through that communion with our Redeemer that we stay aligned with His will. It's not a battle we must fight alone, however. Jesus prayed for us to be protected from the temptations Satan puts on our paths:

> My prayer is not that you take them out of the world but that you protect them from the evil one. They are not of the world, even as I am not of it.
>
> —JOHN 17:15–16

We may sit in church and, when we're supposed to be praying, let our minds drift to other subjects—work, family and money.

Satan is subtle and powerful in his tactics. We can't be preoccupied with the things of this world and still pray. God deserves our undivided attention.

POWER

"Power corrupts, and absolute power corrupts absolutely," a wise man once said. We must rely heavily on our prayers with God to keep us safe from power's lure.

Not even Jesus' disciples were free from the desire for power and positions of authority.

> Then James and John, the sons of Zebedee, came

to him. "Teacher," they said, "we want you to do for us whatever we ask."

"What do you want me to do for you?" he asked.

They replied, "Let one of us sit at your right and the other at your left in your glory."

"You don't know what you are asking," Jesus said. "Can you drink the cup I drink or be baptized with the baptism I am baptized with?"

"We can," they answered.

Jesus said to them, "You will drink the cup I drink and be baptized with the baptism I am baptized with, but to sit at my right or left is not for me to grant. These places belong to those for whom they have been prepared."

When the ten heard about this, they became indignant with James and John. Jesus called them together and said, "You know that those who are regarded as rulers of the Gentiles lord it over them, and their high officials exercise authority over them. Not so with you. Instead, whoever wants to become great among you must be your servant, and whoever wants to be first must be slave of all. For even the Son of Man did not come to be served, but to serve, and to give his life as a ransom for many."

—MARK 10:35–45

We have to continually examine our motives to insure that we desire to serve rather than be in a position of power. God alone has the title of "boss." If our prayer lives are struggles for control of our lives, we don't have true fellowship with God and we aren't His servants.

MATERIAL GOODS

For the love of money is a root of all kinds of evil.
—1 TIMOTHY 6:10

Having money doesn't mean we'll have no prayer life.

Money can be one of the blessings God bestows on us. But when it takes priority in our lives, we no longer give God top billing and our relationship with Him through prayer suffers accordingly.

Money is worshiped in today's society just as it was in New Testament times. The Scriptures are filled with examples of individuals who stored up grain and worried about wealth instead of focusing on Jesus and communing with Him in prayer. In the Gospel of Mark, we are reminded that deceitfulness and covetousness take us away from the Lord:

> But the worries of this life, the deceitfulness of wealth and the desire for other things come in and choke the word, making it unfruitful.
>
> —MARK 4:19

The Book of Acts brings us the tragic story of Ananias and Sapphira. During the time when the power of the Holy Spirit was so mighty, people willingly sold their land and possessions in order to give the money to the Lord's work. No one among these believers lacked anything because of their obedience to God.

Ananias and Sapphira willingly sold their property, but they stumbled when the time came to part with the profits:

> Then Peter said, "Ananias, how is it that Satan has so filled your heart that you have lied to the Holy Spirit and have kept for yourself some of the money you received for the land?...What made you think of doing such a thing? You have not lied to men but to God." When Ananias heard this, he fell down and died.
>
> —ACTS 5:3–5

Sapphira's love of money caused her to follow in the steps of her husband and suffer the same fatal consequences. Focusing on money leads us all far from God.

Yet we can steer clear of the danger associated with the love of money if we devote a good part of our treasure to God.

Things we own—homes, cars, clothes or conveniences—also may distract us from focusing fully on our Lord. To prevent this, we must realize we're only temporary stewards of any possessions, not the true owners. Our Father in heaven owns everything.

Jesus teaches us how to give possessions the appropriate place in our lives:

> Do not store up for yourselves treasures on earth, where moth and rust destroy, and where thieves break in and steal. But store up for yourselves treasures in heaven, where moth and rust do not destroy and where thieves do not break in and steal. For where your treasure is, there your heart will be also.
>
> —MATTHEW 6:19–21

History shows us that all the benefits of prosperity are temporal. All the risks of prosperity are eternal. Matthew 16:26 says, "What good will it be for a man if he gains the whole world, yet forfeits his soul?"

The desire for possessions can lead to behavior that takes us further from the heart of God. Here are the warnings of the prophet Jeremiah:

> "From the least to the greatest, all are greedy for gain; prophets and priests alike, all practice deceit. They dress the wound of my people as though it were not serious. 'Peace, peace,' they say, when there is no peace. Are they ashamed of their loathsome conduct? No, they have no shame at all; they do not even know how to blush. So they will fall among the fallen; they will be brought down when I punish them," says the LORD.
>
> —JEREMIAH 6:13–15

These words hold a special meaning for physicians. We must realize we cannot tell patients not to worry when their wounds are serious. Part of the care and respect we should show our patients is to be lovingly honest with them. Our actions should be the actions of the Lord. Our desires should be those of the Lord. Our "treasure" should not be in a great or prestigious practice, but it should be in serving the Lord and His people.

In Conclusion

Greed, power, control—all will keep us from a true union with God in prayer. Satan can use many temptations to lure us from a lifestyle of prayer. But many thanks be to God, who forgives us when we fail and strengthens us for the next battle.

> One thing God has spoken,
>   two things have I heard:
> that you, O God, are strong,
>   and that you, O Lord, are loving.
>
> —PSALM 62:11–12

Prayer in Action

Chapter Six: Roadblocks to Prayer

For group discussion or personal reflection:

1. What circumstances or problems are the most difficult to give to God to control? What happens to your prayer life during those times?

2. When is your faith the weakest? The strongest?

3. Does it require a lot of discipline for you to pray regularly? Do you look forward to times of prayer?

4. Think about a time when God answered a prayer but in a different way than what you were expecting. What did you learn from the experience?

5. Have you ever been so busy with work, even church work, that you haven't made time to pray? What happened?

6. What are some of the most difficult temptations for you? How do you rely on God's help to fight them off?

7. What possessions or roles of responsibility would be the most difficult for you to give up? Why? Do they play the proper role in your life, or are they too high a priority?

Chapter Seven

DIFFERING VIEWS OF GOD

The way people relate to God is seen through how they pray. And just as no two people are the same, no two people pray in the same way to our Lord. We pray differently because of the differences in our personalities. Some of us are extroverts or introverts in our conversations with our Redeemer, just as we are extroverts or introverts in our relationships with friends and family and in our work. Some of us are more considerate of others; some are more selfish. We also have different fundamental ways of praying. Some are more formal; some, more conversational.

But, we also pray differently because of the differences in the ways we perceive God—whether we think He is all-powerful and yet accessible to us.

TWO VIEWS OF GOD

In theological terms, God is called "transcendent" (above us) and "immanent" (with us). To say God is transcendent means He is eternal, unchangeable and without limits. He is independent and self-existent. God is infinitely greater than all His creatures and infinite in holiness. He is three and yet one. God's transcendence is His greatness.

This greatness stirs wonder, awe and humility in us as His creation. For example, Psalm 147:5 says, "Great is our Lord and mighty in power; his understanding has no limit." And Job 11:7–9 says, "Can you fathom the mysteries of God? Can you probe the limits of the Almighty? They are higher than the heavens—what can you do? They are deeper than the depths of the grave—what can you know? Their measure is longer than the earth and wider than the sea."

To say God is immanent means He is near us as our help and comfort. He sustains us in times of trouble, and we trust and abide in Him as our Lord and Redeemer. Psalm 46:1–3 describes this relationship:

> God is our refuge and strength, an ever-present help in trouble. Therefore we will not fear, though the earth give way and the mountains fall into the heart of the sea, though its waters roar and foam and the mountains quake with their surging.

Some of us would like to separate God's greatness and his nearness—His transcendence and His immanence. Some would say we're removed from God and God is somewhere else. Our prayers become too formal; we don't believe in a personal relationship with Him. We put Him at a distance. Then we try to use that distant God in prayers to do something supernatural, something not based on the sound doctrine of the Word of God.

Some of us look at Him only as a transcendent God way up in the sky—a creator who doesn't have much to do with us now. We think of God as a king who reigns but does not rule, just as English monarchs reign but don't actually govern. However, God is an absolute monarch; He has no external restraints because all authority is in His person.

The Old Testament shows how God reigns over His chosen people, Israel. The New Testament shows how God reigns over the people who believe in His Son, who is exalted to the right hand of authority. God, in His absolute authority, has raised powers and destroyed powers. He is sovereign. He is the ultimate ruler.

Those who want a personal relationship with God and pray say He is immanent. We need to have God with us to receive His power. But if we don't acknowledge His greatness, His transcendence, we limit Him. We don't see the many different faces of God—the Jehovah-Rophe who heals; the Jehovah-Jireh who provides; the Jehovah-Nissi who is the banner; and all the other Jehovahs who make up our Lord. We fail to see the many faces that are present within the Lord that will allow us to pray to Him in a meaningful way.

But He is both with us and above us. If we don't believe in both aspects of God, we don't have an intimate relationship with Him. God is with us as Christ Jesus and the Holy Spirit, and He is greater than us as the Creator, the Father. When we believe that, we can meditate and find ourselves with thoughts that are the Lord's thoughts; we find His Spirit within us. And in a spiritual sense, we're with Him.

When we recognize that God is both greater than we are and near to us, our prayer life is simple. We pray with God just as we would talk with our friends, family or others close to us. We don't need dramatic prayers seeking irrational events. And God doesn't demand prayers that are showy or ostentatious or demanding or pushy.

We need only to direct to the Lord our prayers seeking to bring us closer to Him. We pray quietly, with love and compassion for others, while we are one with the Lord. He becomes our dwelling place. Psalm 34:8 says, "Taste and see that the Lord is good; blessed is the man who takes refuge in him."

LIVING FOR THE MOMENT, OR LIVING FOR GOD?

We pray differently when we don't think about heaven, but only here and now. When we believe that this time is all there is, that there's nothing else, no supernatural realm, then we act as though anything goes. We become pagans, saying this is all there is, so we should enjoy it.

We then lose our close contact with God; we may even quit praying altogether. We become isolated from Him.

And then we're alienated and estranged from the world, God's creation, and from God, the Creator. And, once we're alienated from God, we have no relationships. We're alienated from ourselves, from others, from nature and from institutions such as government. We want to get as much out of this life as possible, because we begin to believe that this life is all there is.

Our prayers, if we pray at all in this frame of mind, are pragmatic. They are prayers for things to help in our daily lives, for events of the day to work out well. We focus on asking for results rather than seeking a growing relationship with God. We ask, we demand, and we feel cheated when those demands aren't granted.

We acknowledge God only when we see evidence of Him at work. We pray for phenomena, for things we can see, because we care only for scientific observations and rational behavior. We don't have the faith to know He is always at work in our lives.

We must learn to know that God is always with us, even when we don't see Him. We should seek to align ourselves with God, to develop a relationship with Him based not on results but on love and faith.

A Picture out of Focus

We frequently picture God as we see ourselves, which means we picture God incorrectly. We make up a God who either is laid-back or productive, a God who is friendly or a God who is legalistic. We do not then worship the God of Calvary, the God of surrender and forgiveness. We must be careful that we worship a true picture of God. If our picture of God reflects our picture of ourselves, we are then worshiping ourselves rather than our Creator and Redeemer.

If we picture God based on how we see ourselves, we can't accept people who are not like us. We make up gods in our world that are like us, and we are not lenient with those that are not like us. By staying in the Word of God and by being guided by the Holy Spirit, we follow closely in its steps, staying close to the true God.

It's important what God we choose to worship because we gradually become like the God we worship. "Whatever then the heart clings to, whatever the heart relies on, that is properly thy God," Martin Luther said.

The Need for Unity

I want men everywhere to lift up holy hands in prayer, without anger or disputing.

—1 Timothy 2:8

I appeal to you, brothers, in the name of our Lord Jesus Christ, that all of you agree with one another so that there may be no divisions among you and that you may be perfectly united in mind and thought.

—1 Corinthians 1:10

In spite of the diversity of the ways we pray, unity still is important. There's a story about two cars, coming from opposite directions, crashing into each other. It was a horrible disaster. Many people lost their lives, and as survivors and rescue workers searched the accident scene they realized one little girl was missing. They split up and searched for her in every direction, thinking she might have been thrown from the car.

After several hours, she still had not been found. So the search party decided to join hands to comb the fields in the pasture around the accident. The area was vast and it was tough going, but within half an hour they yelled, "We found her!" A doctor came over, examined the girl and told everyone she was dead, but that she hadn't been dead long.

Her father, who had lived through the crash, said, "If we'd only put our hands together, had been more in unity earlier, we could have saved her. If we hadn't gone our own ways but had joined hands sooner we could have found her and saved her."

This is so true of the Church of Jesus Christ today. We must join hands and work and pray together to do God's will on this earth. It's only when we're aligned with God that the Church will advance.

Prayer in Action

Chapter Seven: Differing Views of God

For group discussion or personal reflection:

1. What does God's transcendence mean to you? His immanence?

2. Does God seem more immanent or more transcendent to you?

3. When do your prayers focus merely on results? Why?

4. How much of yourself do you see in your perception of God?

5. How does your view of God get out of focus?

6. Have you ever been part of a group that prayed with a united vision of God? How did your individual prayer life change?

7. How did dissent change the group?

Chapter Eight

The Developing Prayer Life

You do not have, because you do not ask God.

—James 4:2

Most of us pray only when all else fails. We need to have a regular, earnest and persistent prayer life. Our prayer should be more than a few words each day. It should be embodied within us, changing us.

We must not be content with where we are spiritually. The Lord God wants us to continue to grow in our understanding of love for Him. That is why we must press on by daily surrender in prayers. Worshipful prayer goes beyond a mere daily routine. The Lord would like to guide us during every step of our day; all we have to do is listen to Him. Watching and praying enable us to hear His voice clearly. Then we get to know the heart of God, to become more intimate with Him.

We go through three stages as we develop our prayer life. First, we're disciplined in our prayers, then our prayer becomes heartfelt and, finally, our whole beings are consumed by our relationship in prayer with the Lord.

Disciplined Prayer

Prayer requires discipline. We discipline our bodies to become athletes. In the same way, it's important to focus on growing closer to God through prayer. It requires practice and effort—conditioning. The disciplined prayer life is when we set up times for just praying. It may be liturgical prayer or conversational prayer, but we begin to develop a discipline with praying.

It always has been easier for me to improve the condition of my body than to bring my soul into subjection. It is much easier for me to *do* things for the Lord than to *submit* to Him—to recognize Him as all-important and sovereign. It is a discipline to align ourselves to be with God and only God, to be intimate with Him, to know Him and for Him to know us. This is the intimacy of being a Christian.

Focusing on what I do best has enabled me to become more fervent in my prayer. Christians are commanded to fight slothfulness and to be faithful and focused. It is important to do one thing at a time and to do it well. In my ophthalmology practice, I have worked hard to narrow my specialty and remain focused on procedures I do best and with fewer complications. The days that I have the most work on my calendar are the days I need to pray more. Days that I am disciplined and make a stronger effort to pray and stay in the Word are the days that flow in my life.

HEARTFELT PRAYER

> I will praise the LORD, who counsels me; even at night my heart instructs me. I have set the LORD always before me. Because he is at my right hand, I will not be shaken.
>
> —PSALM 16:7–8

Many people in the Bible were disciplined and set aside three times to pray during the day. Even the old Jewish prayers were not enough, and in the New Testament the disciples asked, "Lord, teach us to pray." They realized the disciplined prayer life of the Old Testament wasn't adequate.

So the second stage is taking prayer beyond the times we set aside and making prayer an integral part of our daily lives. Just as the motor skills we use to play sports or do our jobs become ingrained responses, so it should

be with our prayer lives. We have an increasing awareness of God and our need for His direction daily in our
lives. Our active faith in God is reflected in a soul
engaged in constant meditation with our Redeemer. Our
hearts are so directed toward God that we are being
directed by Him and not by the world.

Our prayers now become heartfelt. Everything that is
within us cries out for the Lord. The joy that comes from
our relationship with the Lord overcomes us. When we
know God as both immanent (near us) and transcendent
(all powerful), our prayer lives are constant. It is just like
talking to another person on earth.

A variety of thoughts go between us and the Lord, and
the Lord is one with us. We don't have to pray in showy,
ostentatious, demanding or pushy ways. We simply think
and talk to the Lord.

We're not looking for dramatic events to give us more
faith in God. We're merely in communion with our
closest friend. That relationship gives us peace and a
sense of joy and purpose as we live our lives on earth.

WHOLESELF PRAYER

> O God, you are my God, earnestly I seek you; my
> soul thirsts for you, my body longs for you.
>   —PSALM 63:1

When every bit of energy we have is turned toward the
Lord, we've reached the third stage—wholeself prayer.
Everything we have and we are is in prayer. The prayerful
spirit becomes so pervasive in our lives that our souls are
intertwined with prayer. Prayer becomes so integrated in
our lives that it is like dew. Our lives are scented by it.
Our prayers extend not just in our heads but throughout
our bodies.

Richard Foster writes about a pilgrim, a Russian
peasant who prayed in his head so much that the prayer
became part of his heart and went throughout his body.

Foster's breath prayers are examples of the thoughts that extend through our whole being: "Lord, baptize me with love." "Teach me gentleness, Father." "Teach me patience, Father." "Lord Jesus, help me feel loved and help me love."

Prayer in Action

Chapter Eight: The Developing Prayer Life

For group discussion or personal reflection:

1. Are you happy with your prayer life? Does it need changing?

2. How can you build a stronger prayer life? What are some practical tools that will help you?

3. Are you a disciplined prayer? If not, how can you build that discipline into your daily routine?

4. Have there been times when you've been in heartfelt prayer? Describe the feeling.

5. When have your prayers extended through your whole being? How did that happen?

6. Richard Foster's breath prayers are one tool to building a stronger prayer life. How would you use them in your life?

CHAPTER NINE

A NEW LIFE

Through prayer we grow in the likeness of God, and our moral character changes. When we accept Christ as our Savior, we accept His holiness that comes from grace. But our character changes as we become obedient through studying His Word, being filled with the Holy Spirit and praying.

Bill Hybels, a pastor in the Chicago area, sums up this change well. He says that Christians are supernatural people who walk with a living, dynamic, communicating God. We move to a different drummer. We have a deeper character and ideas that are fresher. Our spirit is softer, our courage is greater, our leadership is stronger, our concerns are wider, our compassion is genuine and generous, and our joy doesn't depend on circumstances.

Prayer changes our inner disposition and transforms everything. "When we pray, things remain the same, but we begin to be different," Oswald Chambers wrote in *If You Will Ask.* "Prayer is not altering things externally, but working wonders within our disposition."

We have to remember that the Lord doesn't always want to change our circumstances. God wants to change our character. The way He changes our character is through the things that happen to us. We are changed through our decisions—particularly during the toughest trials—to align ourselves with the world or to align ourselves with Him. When we become aligned with God, our priorities change.

The life of a man named George Mueller shows us how a life can be changed when it is aligned with God. Mueller dedicated his life to helping orphaned children in England. Knowing that God had called him to that particular ministry, Mueller depended entirely upon His support. Mueller never asked for money. He relied on prayer and developed the following daily prayer vigil:

Each day he read his Bible with expectation until he came upon something especially meaningful to him. He always read believing that God would give him a specific word for the day. When God did, Mueller wrote down what it meant to him. Then he meditated on the significance of the Scriptures he had read and examined his thoughts, allowing the Holy Spirit to bring His ultimate purpose into focus. Finally, he spoke to someone about what he had learned and how it related to him.

George Mueller became accustomed to starting each day this way. A deep, full life of prayer and worship of God changed his life. Our lives also can be changed by a growing relationship with God.

Thomas Aquinas noted that persistence in prayer consisted not of asking for many things, but of desiring one thing—God Himself. This steadfastness brings about change in every parameter of our existence.

Prayer that inclines us to God's will establishes order in a once-fragmented life, because God is the author of order, not confusion.

INNER DISPOSITION

> If your outward actions are a result (a by-product) of something that has taken place deep within you, then those outward actions do receive spiritual value and they do possess real goodness. But outward activities have only as much spiritual value as they receive from their source.
> —MADAME JEANNE GUYON, 1685

Our inner disposition as we pray is important. The apostle Paul preached about the internal versus the external person. Being authentic on the external side of our lives depends on our internal relationship with God.

A key element in my own spiritual journey to become an authentic Christian has been the issue of inward disposition. Through my days, I try to stop and measure whether I am allowing my heavenly affections to permeate my inner disposition as I live and care for others, including patients.

As I experience the depths of Jesus Christ in my life, I experience changes in my inner disposition. Being an inner person requires contemplation and allowing the Lord into my life as I treat patients, talk to my wife, negotiate business contracts and so on. In her book, *Experiencing the Depths of Jesus Christ*, Madame Guyon compared the struggle to develop the inner person to a ship on its way out to sea. At first, the crew members must use all their strength to get the vessel to clear the harbor. But once at sea, the ship sails freely and easily in whatever direction the seamen choose.

About a hundred years later, in the late 1700s Jonathan Edwards made some of the same observations about the inner person. He said that true religion, in a great part, consists in holy affections. What we are alive to internally is what we are inclined toward outwardly. For example, people who are alive internally to sports activities are interested in all types of sports. Other people are dead internally to sports and therefore are not interested in those activities. They are not so inclined.

The same holds true for our heavenly affections and our love for Christ. True prayer, as described in the works of Edwards, is an active inclination to God. Deuteronomy 6:5 tells us: "Love the Lord your God with all your heart and with all your soul and with all your strength."

I believe that the inner disposition is born out of real love for Jesus Christ and out of devotion to His teachings. Praying, reading Scripture, asking forgiveness and being focused on the Lord Jesus are tools that keep me on the path to achieving that authentic external personality.

Praising the Lord also helps me to realize heavenly affections in my day-to-day life. Some people begin each prayer by thanking the Lord for the list of victories and defeats in their daily lives.

I don't think it matters how you praise the Lord. But I know that it changes your mind-set, your soul and your inclination so that you rejoice in the Lord. Rejoicing in God allows my outward actions to receive spiritual value and possess real goodness.

As we relate to Jesus in a contemplative and prayerful way, we allow Him to communicate with us. We also can develop an inner peace and inner confidence through His grace. Seeking to be with Christ and worshiping Him on the cross should be our first goal. Developing an inner disposition is the first step to reaching that objective.

A SPIRIT-FILLED LIFE

> Those who live according to the sinful nature have their minds set on what that nature desires; but those who love in accordance with the Spirit have their minds set on what the Spirit desires.
>
> —ROMANS 8:5

As our prayers are lifted up to God and we're aligned with Him, we become one with Him in sincerity. Then we receive an abundant supply of the Holy Spirit. Paul refers to this supply in his letter from prison to the Philippians, using the word *epichoregia*. It means an abundant supply sufficient for an army.

That abundant supply of the Spirit results in our salvation and deliverance past, present and future. God's Word tells us about our deliverance in the past in Ephesians 2:8–9:

> For it is by grace you have been saved, through faith—and this not from yourselves, it is the gift of God—not by works, so that no one can boast.

For our salvation and deliverance in the present we're told in 1 Corinthians 1:18, "For the message of the cross is foolishness to those who are perishing, but to us who are being saved it is the power of God."

Our future deliverance is assured in 2 Timothy 4:18: "The Lord will rescue me from every evil attack and will bring me safely to his heavenly kingdom. To him be glory for ever and ever. Amen."

When we are filled with that abundance of the Holy Spirit our lives can never be the same. Paul's letter to a group of churches in Galatia tells them, and us, to live by the Spirit, to be led by the Spirit and to keep in step with the Spirit. And Galatians 5:22–23 spells out some of the characteristics of that new life:

> But the fruit of the Spirit is love, joy, peace, patience, kindness, goodness, faithfulness, gentleness and self-control. Against such things there is no law.

Strengthened Lives

> The LORD is with me; I will not be afraid. What can man do to me?
>
> —Psalm 118:6

A lifestyle of unceasing prayer can strengthen our lives. In his book, *Prayer*, Richard J. Foster says, "Unceasing prayer has a way of speaking peace to the chaos. We begin experiencing something of the cosmic patience of God. Our fractured and fragmented activities begin focusing around a new Center of Reference. We experience peace, stillness, serenity, firmness of life orientation."

Foster suggests that prayers can be connected to routine things in our lives. Surgeons, he said, can pray every time they scrub before an operation. Others can pray whenever they see their favorite color or during a regular daily activity.

Foster calls those moments "holy habits" that "will do their work of integration so that praying becomes the easy thing, the natural thing, the spontaneous thing." The difficult thing, he says, "will be to refrain from prayer."

MEDITATION ON THE WORD

Meditation on God's Word as it applies in our lives is critical as we attempt to have a mind of prayer.

For example, I recite 1 Corinthians 13 every day because I think my deficit is in loving and caring for people. I want to be sure I am sincerely loving and caring.

> If I speak in the tongues of men and of angels, but have not love, I am only a resounding gong or a clanging cymbal. If I have the gift of prophecy and can fathom all mysteries and all knowledge, and if I have a faith that can move mountains, but have not love, I am nothing. If I give all I possess to the poor and surrender my body to the flames, but have not love, I gain nothing.
>
> Love is patient, love is kind. It does not envy, it does not boast, it is not proud. It is not rude, it is not self-seeking, it is not easily angered, it keeps no record of wrongs. Love does not delight in evil but rejoices with the truth. It always protects, always trusts, always hopes, always perseveres.
>
> Love never fails. But where there are prophecies, they will cease; where there are tongues, they will be stilled; where there is knowledge, it will pass away. For we know in part and we prophesy in part, but when perfection comes, the imperfect disappears. When I was a child, I talked like a child, I thought like a child, I reasoned like a child. When I became a man, I put childish ways behind me. Now we see but a poor reflection as in a mirror; then we shall see face to face. Now I know in part; then I shall know fully, even as I am

fully known.

And now these three remain: faith, hope and love. But the greatest of these is love.

I take the word *patient* and ask myself whether I am patient with other people, whether I am patient with the Lord, whether I am patient with life. Then I take the word *kind* and ask myself whether I am kind to others, whether I am kind to the people with whom I work.

We need to take each word of the Scripture and see whether it applies to our lives. When it doesn't, our prayer lives can suffer. Meditation on God's Word helps us stay inclined to God and in communion with Him through prayer.

A Deeper Faith

The degree of faith we have in God is the degree to which we are at rest and at peace. As we grow closer to our Redeemer, our level of trust and faith increases. We understand more fully that God's faithfulness is total and that He doesn't change. James 1:17 says, "Every good and perfect gift is from above, coming down from the Father of the heavenly lights, who does not change like shifting shadows."

Much of faith is learning how to hang in and hold on, knowing the Lord is our partner. Hebrews 11:1 gives us a definition of faith: "Now faith is being sure of what we hope for and certain of what we do not see." The rest of Chapter 11 cites example after example of faith in action—the faith of Noah, Abraham, Moses and many others. These examples can help build our faith when we're feeling out of faith.

Faith determines how close we are to God. And as our faith increases, so does our confidence and trust in God to meet our needs. That builds on itself. We trust in God; He provides. When we see that He provides, we trust even more. And we rely on those examples of how

He provides when times are tough. He gives us those examples of faith in action so we can continue to lean on Him and not on ourselves.

A LIFESTYLE OF SURRENDER

One of the most important changes in our lives is our surrender of ourselves to God. A surrendered life is necessary to walk more deeply with Christ and to welcome in the fullness of the Holy Spirit. The surrendered life separates those whose desires are for what God wants from those who have their own agendas.

In the twenty-third Psalm, David describes the anointing that comes from prayer, the knowledge that the Lord is with us. Individuals who truly have been anointed through prayer admit to the sovereignty of God. When we do that we can live a life of a passionate prayer to the Father. We have no cares, having cast them upon the Lord. We trust in God above all things. And then we're blessed with many fruits of the Spirit, including joy, peace and patience, because we know God will supply what we need.

Anointed children of God have surrendered and submitted to the Lord. They have voluntarily subjected themselves to the authority of God. They have taken away their pride, which interferes with their relationship with God. And they are able to allow the Lord to direct their lives through reading His Word, praying and having worshipful attitudes.

In my journey to know and imitate Jesus Christ, I often have struggled with the answer to the question: "Am I striving to be sanctified for the greater glory of God, or the glory of my patients, peers and admirers?" Through a long process of surrendering my own desires and will to the Lord, He has allowed our work at St. Luke's Cataract and Laser Institute to flourish.

Medicine is a place where we simply serve. Most doctors

experience that personal call when they begin to practice. But so often our pride and our egos and our own agendas interfere with patient care. It is common in Christian dialogue to talk about surrendering to Jesus. But we also must surrender to our patients and surrender to being doctors. To be caring people, we have to give up things that normally motivate us and live a lifestyle of surrender.

BEING A SERVANT

> Whoever wants to become great among you must be your servant, and whoever wants to be first must be your slave—just as the Son of Man did not come to be served, but to serve, and to give his life as a ransom for many.
>
> —MATTHEW 20:26–27

After we surrender our agendas and desires to God, we must also surrender ourselves to others as God's servants on earth. As the Lord came to earth to serve and not be served, we must follow His example.

Jesus, the master, washed the disciples' feet. We must bring the same attitude of servanthood and humility to our lives. We must surrender ourselves to be people who delight in washing others' feet, caring for the most mundane parts of a human being.

A LIFESTYLE OF CARING

> Then make my joy complete by being like-minded, having the same love, being one in spirit and purpose. Do nothing out of selfish ambition or vain conceit, but in humility consider others better than yourselves. Each of you should look not only to your own interests, but also to the interests of others. Your attitude should be the same as that of Christ Jesus.
>
> —PHILIPPIANS 2:2–5

Unless we are properly aligned with God and put our

priorities right through prayer, we cannot surrender ourselves so we can be compassionate and caring with
others. As a doctor, it is a privilege for me to care for
God's people.

But service without love is hollow. He wants all of us
at St. Luke's to be totally tied in a caring relationship
with our patients, giving of ourselves and letting ourselves be submitted to them in every way. All of us must
be able to love others in the manner in which God would
have us love.

I know that spending time in prayer changes how I
relate to people. I let God's love be reflected through me.
My wife, Heather, uses the word *considerate*. I like the
word *appreciative* as well. We appreciate our families
and our jobs; we appreciate our coworkers, clients and
customers; we appreciate a certain situation the Lord has
left us in; we appreciate even those seventy-hour work
weeks because we serve the Lord through love.

We can be like the moon. We can be cold and not have
much intrinsically to offer others. It is only the reflection
of sunlight that gives the moon value to us on earth. In
the same way, we must let the Son of God be reflected
through us. Our lives must reflect Jesus and His love to
have any permanent value and eternal significance. Our
own efforts are not important.

> And we, who with unveiled faces all reflect the
> Lord's glory, are being transformed into his like-
> ness with ever-increasing glory, which comes
> from the Lord, who is the Spirit.
>
> —2 CORINTHIANS 3:18

We have to be on guard to make sure we are caring for
others with the right motives. If we are going to truly care
for people, we must get away from coveting, because coveting destroys our ability to function and focus.
Whenever we covet, be it material things or a symbol of
success such as a position of authority, we no longer can

see clearly. We become selfish, coveting for our own gain, not honoring God. And our prayer life dries up. "If a man shuts his ears to the cry of the poor, he too will cry out and not be answered," Proverbs 21:13 says.

So coveting keeps us from being able to truly worship God and to have an intimate relationship with Him. And we cannot care for others without that relationship with our Lord.

For example, a doctor who wants only possessions works for money and for the material things it buys. He does not look at his patients but looks at what he can receive from them. He may indeed produce good medical care, but not to the degree he's fully capable of. And he isn't serving and worshiping God when he cares for people. He may make a lot of money and do a good job practicing medicine, but his inward inclination isn't toward God.

Let's look at another example. Say there's a doctor who wants to have the biggest practice in the world. This doctor will see more and more patients and give each of them less and less time. The doctor will see so many patients that he truly can't relate to others and he may not even give them good medical care.

In any profession, not just medicine, we must think about our final goal. Is it to covet or to care? Is our bottom line just theological or practical? Do we care for people? Are we compassionate with them? Are they our top priority? Can we listen to their complaints? Can we be humble so we can be servants?

As I've talked to physicians with large practices, I'm amazed at how many of them have developed a sense of caring through prayer and surrender of self. They take on an inner disposition that allows them to care for others. Some of these physicians are among the top in the world, yet their work is easy, not difficult. Because they spend most of their time in prayer, their work becomes a natural and pleasant manifestation of the outpouring of the Holy Spirit.

A nurse I know at St. Luke's genuinely cares about others and is a real encourager. Her name is Angel, and she has children with quite a few learning disabilities. With her encouragement, her children have matured and become self-supporting. Her youngest daughter also became a competitive runner sought by some of the best universities in the country. Angel's encouragement led her family to flourish.

We won't change people by our words; they will be changed by the way prayer changes us. Practicing medicine is about that change. Our words or actions will not change our patients; they are changed by the way prayer changes us. They are treated through our compassion for them. That compassion comes only from the Lord—the Healer.

The encouragement and caring we provide patients often carries them through the procedures better than the medicines we prescribe. It is natural for patients to worry, and it's important for doctors to realize that they have very realistic fears.

Fear is the biggest disease we treat. A good percentage of patients are really scared when they come to our clinic. I can tell them, "Don't worry; everything will be all right." But they won't hear that. The one phrase that seems to break through is, "I understand."

Understanding and caring go hand in hand. Building on that caring relationship with a patient is an annuity. From then on, that patient will remember your kindness. He will refer his friends to your practice—perhaps when business is slow.

Those conversations with patients, those encouraging and understanding words, reflect the quality of the patient's medical care.

> Yet on the day of your fasting, you do as you please and exploit all your workers...You cannot fast as you do today and expect your voice to be heard on high...Is not this the kind of fasting I have chosen: to loose the chains of injustice and untie the cords of the yoke, to set the oppressed free and break every yoke? Is it not to share your food with the hungry and to provide the poor wanderer with shelter—when you see the naked, to clothe him, and not to turn away from your own flesh and blood?...Then you will call, and the Lord will answer; you will cry for help, and he will say: Here am I.
>
> —ISAIAH 58:3–4, 6–7, 9

When we fast, we refrain from something. Those to whom God was speaking in Isaiah refrained from doing good works, and continued to practice hypocrisy and injustice.

God tells us He wants us to turn from our evil ways. We should not be condemning one another; we should be evaluating our own lives and then serving others with a right spirit. When we freely and cheerfully keep that kind of fast, we receive many blessings and benefits from our Redeemer and Creator.

God wants us to have a softer spirit as we deal with others, just as He loves and cares for us. Once we've surrendered ourselves to Him, serving others with care and compassion comes more naturally.

When we have His Spirit in us, we are guided by His love and the fruit of the Spirit—love, joy, peace, patience, kindness, goodness, faithfulness, gentleness and self-control. Those are but a natural progression as we grow in our relationship with our Lord through prayer.

PRAYER IN ACTION

CHAPTER NINE: A NEW LIFE

For group discussion or personal reflection:

1. George Mueller gives us an example of applying God's Word to a lifestyle of prayer. How can you apply this example in your life?

2. Has your prayer life changed your inner disposition? How?

3. Do you see the fruit of the Spirit in your life? Which are the greatest in your life? Which are the least?

4. Read Chapter 11 of Hebrews. How do the stories of faith affect your faith?

5. Is there a special Scripture passage that speaks to you? How do you meditate on it and apply it in your life?

6. Is it difficult to serve others? Is it more difficult to serve those you know or those you don't know?

7. When do you have the right motives for helping others? The wrong motives? What makes the difference?

CHAPTER TEN

FAMILY FELLOWSHIP

I was going to work the other day and I stopped by to visit with a neighbor, a former patient of mine, who was out in his front yard with his little white dog. The man told me he had just put his wife in an Alzheimer's unit because he could no longer give her around-the-clock care at home.

While we talked, his lips quivered and his eyes shifted, looking to me and then away. While his wife had a disease, he had a "dis-ease" about life. We spoke about our love for our spouses and our love for God. At the end of the road of life, those loves become even more important.

That conversation made me wonder why I didn't appreciate my wife enough and why I let little things irritate me. I'm sure every spouse has been in a similar situation—we criticize and are irritated by those with whom we've pledged to build a life.

Yet it's impossible for any one person to make another person feel full. We all have come up short for our partner. We must then ask blessings for our spouse and forgiveness for ourselves. As we are faithful, fervent and focused in loving God, so we should be with our spouse. A marriage relationship that is out of synch can affect our relationship with God. For how can we love God if we don't act out of love with our husband or wife? If we're not aligned through love with our spouse, can we be aligned through love with our Creator?

The Bible says a great deal about family relationships. Marriage symbolizes the union between Jesus and His Bride, the Church. Thus, He expects husbands to love their wives the way He loves the Church, and wives to revere their husbands the way the Church reverences

Him. If the relationship between husband and wife doesn't have that love and respect, our relationship with God may lack the same thing. And our prayer life suffers.

> Husbands, in the same way be considerate as you live with your wives, and treat them with respect as the weaker partner and as heirs with you of the gracious gift of life, so that nothing will hinder your prayers.
>
> —1 PETER 3:7

We must fight the constant pull by the world that tempts us to criticize, to judge, to be irritated by our spouses and ask God's blessings for our husband or wife. If we pray for our husband or wife at the times that we would normally be mad, the anger, resentment and hostility are diffused by God's love for us and our love for each other.

The way to maintain a strong relationship with our spouse is to love God with all our heart and to be a channel of His love to our spouse.

"As you share in prayer with your wife and children, and as you mature in the ways of Christ, you will find a new meaning to family life," Dr. Juan Batlle says. "You should try in every possible way to witness to your spouse, children and to other family members. As your testimony is strengthened, your life is slowly transformed."

Through my son Pit's teenage years I decided rather than arguing and telling him what to do, we would pray together and look in the Bible for the answer to a specific problem. We looked for the answer that was best for him, for society and for all of us.

Our families are blessings from God. When there is strife in the family, we may focus on that rather than on God. But we cannot heal any family divisions by ourselves. As we endeavor to truly love our family, we must seek the Lord's guidance and follow His example of loving the Church. So it's important to lift up our family members in prayer, seeking God's blessing upon them and asking His guidance as we build our marriage and raise our children.

PRAYER IN ACTION

CHAPTER TEN: FAMILY FELLOWSHIP

For group discussion or personal reflection:

1. Do you set aside time regularly to pray with your spouse? With your family?

2. How does praying with your spouse and other family members change your relationship with them?

3. Do you use prayer and Bible study to resolve family conflicts? Why or why not?

4. Do you pray regularly for the members of your family? Are you specific in your prayers for them?

5. One way for spouses to pray together is to bless each other. Have you done that? What happened?

CHAPTER ELEVEN

JOY IN THE WORKPLACE

A coworker was telling me that he noticed certain people always were worried about what they were doing at work. Their worries were a huge load on their shoulders. He talked about how he was free from that load and he simply enjoyed work. His prayer life took away the attitude of work as work, and it gave him confidence that the work he was doing was the work God wanted him to do.

By turning our lives over to God we take away the problems of the world because we don't have to worry about them. When we align ourselves with God, we simply turn those problems over to Him and enjoy everything we do. Because of our relationship with Him, represented in prayer, our lives are vibrant and enjoyable.

We've talked about how faithful, fervent and focused prayer changes us: We are filled with the Holy Spirit and surrender ourselves to God. Once we do that, all our attitudes toward life change and we become humble servants who love and care for others as Christ loves and cares for us.

One of the places where the change in our lives should be the most obvious is the workplace. The question is how do we do that?

Sometimes that issue can even become a roadblock to prayer. Do I post a Christian symbol or hang a picture with a Scripture quote? Or would that drive business away? As a doctor, do I offer to pray with patients or do I let my staff members do all that "mushy" stuff? Will I lose business from Jewish patients if I mention Jesus' name? Do I touch the patients in prayer—laying my hands on their eyes—or pray with my arms outstretched? Will I make people feel uncomfortable? And, ultimately, will I drive them away?

If we're afraid of losing business, we'll just say, "I'll operate my business as a professional, and I will worship God on Sundays when I go to church." But that isn't the lifestyle to which God calls us. Just as prayer changes us in our lives outside the office, we should be changed in our work and our attitudes toward it. If we don't live lives of surrender and caring at work, can we truly live it at home? Or are we once again serving two masters?

Bringing the Lord to work does not have to be complicated. It just has to be constant.

BRINGING GOD TO WORK

A very significant way to honor the Lord is to bring Him into the workplace. First there are the conscious means to help us remember to seek Him in prayer during our workday. We can put up notes that remind us of His presence. We can bring a Bible to work to study His Word and pray during breaks or lunch times. We can speak about Him with our coworkers. We can pray for His will as we face challenges and praise Him when work goes well.

Prayer is of the heart; it doesn't have to be of the voice. At St. Luke's we may say things such as, "The Lord's blessing be upon you," so a patient knows we are in prayer without being formal about it. We are merely surrendered in prayer as we see patients. And we are thankful for and blessed by good outcomes for our patients.

But these conscious acts are not enough. We should be in constant communion with Him throughout our work day. That will be reflected in our actions. Ask yourself the question, "Under whose authority do I actually work?" and see how your actions reflect your answer. Do we act as though we don't work for anybody? Are we too proud and independent in our work lives to give God control of our actions at work?

> But the wisdom that comes from heaven is first of
> all pure; then peace-loving, considerate, submis-
> sive, full of mercy and good fruit, impartial and
> sincere.
>
> —JAMES 3:17

Are we pure and do we use pure language? Do we have an attitude of peacekeeping? Do we show mercy? These are the attitudes toward others and toward our work that reflect our active relationship with God through prayer.

LOVING GOD AS WE WORK

Loving God and praying while you work is like being madly in love with your spouse and still playing tennis. Certainly your mind is at peace because you have a love affair with your spouse. Your relationship with and trust in him or her gives you great peace to play tennis. While you concentrate on the tennis match, you're still in love with your spouse. And this love relationship changes you.

The same is true of our relationship with the Lord. It's important to remember to be in love with God con-stantly, as we work and as we play. The conscious acts help us do that. Frequent prayer helps us remember Him. By building that base, we can do many other things and concentrate on them as the love affair we have with God changes us.

This change is greater. His love changes us more than our love affair with our spouse. It's possible to pray, to be changed and still carry out your work.

When our work is centered in prayer, we have godly affections, love, hope, courage and joy in our work. Our love for God changes our approach to work and our atti-tudes toward those with whom we work. It also gives us perspective on how to best accomplish our worldly responsibilities and enrich our spiritual lives at the same time.

It can be so easy to block out our love relationship with our spouse by being too busy with work or other activities. In the same way, it's easy to block out the Lord by letting work or other activities or relationships take top priority. We give our time and energy to those, rather than to the Lord. How we pray determines our priorities, so we must remember to be in faithful, focused and fervent prayer with God.

Each sphere of our life demands its own attention at appropriate times. Those activities require our immediate concentration. How do we keep close to God at the same time?

If we've built a lifestyle of prayer, we've built a solid, strong relationship with God that helps us keep Him in our hearts all the time. Then we can give 100 percent to other areas when it's necessary.

WORK THAT HONORS GOD

But loving God and bringing Him to work isn't all. We honor our Redeemer at work not only by being inclined to Him through prayer, but also by doing a good job in our work. If we claim to do our work in His name but perform shoddy work, how does that glorify our Creator?

Colossians 3:17 says, "Whatever you do, whether in word or deed, do it all in the name of the Lord Jesus, giving thanks to God the Father through him." We must do a good job in all we do, and we must do everything in the name of the Lord. Loving God is a full-time job, but it's accomplished by doing a job of excellence with godly love.

Author David Seamands discusses three levels of life. In the first, we're driven by our desires and urges. In the second, work, duty and religion often are drudgery. In the highest level, law and love are mixed up so that life is a matter of love. We love our work; we love the people with whom we work. This becomes a Spirit-filled level, and duty becomes devotion and joy. We end up delighting in our work. It's important that, through prayer, we know God and know His strengths. Then we will have the freedom to do our work. Jesus says in John 8:32, "You will know the truth and the truth will set you free."

This means we should pray to make our work a product of our desire to serve our Lord. Our work should not be motivated by our desire to prove ourselves or win acceptance or make money so we can accumulate possessions. When we stay faithful, fervent and focused on Jesus, the rest of our lives stay in focus. When we stay focused on the Lord in prayer, we stay focused in our work because we don't think about things that aren't important. We focus on God and seek to honor Him and do His will.

We should also remember that we honor Him by an ethical attitude toward work. Bill Hybels suggests four criteria to determine whether something is ethical: Does it glorify God? Does it benefit His Kingdom? Does it help others? Does it bring us closer to our Redeemer?

As I make my daily rounds at St. Luke's, I try to think of Christ as my boss and I ask myself, "What would Jesus say about my work life? Would He be happy with it?" I know that the Lord is happy when we honor Him in the workplace.

I honor Jesus in my workplace, first, by the way I talk to staff members. Getting along with colleagues is a good place to start. Regardless of their age or their level of experience, God commands us to love one another. Loving means respecting one another.

Author and preacher Chuck Swindoll talks a lot about colleagues. Whether we are children or professionals, he says, we can fall prey to four common pitfalls: to control, to compare, to compete and to criticize. We need to be in control, he explains, because our egos, our psyche, our security or our personal aggrandizement depend on control. Although the Lord tells us to serve others, we have a need to control them instead. We also like to compare. Swindoll defines comparing as being envious and jealous—two things we are warned about in one of Paul's letters to the church at Corinth:

> Some of you have become arrogant, as if I were not coming to you. But I will come to you very soon, if the Lord is willing, and then I will find out not only how these arrogant people are talking, but what power they have. For the kingdom of God is not a matter of talk but of power.
>
> —1 CORINTHIANS 4:18–20

> Love is patient, love is kind. It does not envy, it does not boast, it is not proud.
>
> —1 CORINTHIANS 13:4

I am convinced that the desire to be a good worker and to accomplish career goals can only be accomplished with Jesus.

"I find that when I can maintain a degree of prayerful consciousness while going through the day's activities, I enjoy life and work more," Dr. Dan G. Montgomery of Inverness, Florida, says. "If when presented with an 'unlovely' patient, an unexpected complication or the latest 'gloom and doom' report on oppressive government regulation, I can remember to continue an attitude of background prayer awareness, it helps keep things in perspective.

"I can be thankful to the Lord for allowing me to serve Him in the form of my patients," Dr. Montgomery says. "I can remain calm and steady under the stress of a tough surgical problem in the operating room. And when financial worries loom, prayer reminds me of what is really important. It always surprises me to hear it, but now and then someone will remark that I have a reputation as being relatively steady, calm and unflustered. That's not my nature, I can tell you; it must be the Lord working in me."

INTERCESSION AT WORK AND IN PRACTICE

The basis of our prayer life should be intercession—to go between. Intercession describes one who yields himself among those who are weak and need assistance. It means getting involved in the needs and hurts of others. As the Good Samaritan got involved helping the beaten man by the side of the road, so we should get involved with others.

Before we can pray with others, however, we have to clear our own relationship with the Lord. That includes asking Him for forgiveness and making friends with our enemies. One of the most important things necessary for physicians is that we must purify ourselves before we go into the operating room. We must wash our hands and put on a sterile gown and gloves before we do surgery.

We also have to purify ourselves spiritually. We need to ask the Lord to be washed by the blood of Christ. We need to make Him totally pre-eminent within our lives, being nourished by the Holy Spirit so our minds are in a state of prayer or in the Word all the time.

First Peter 5:7 says, "Cast all your anxiety on him because he cares for you." In a similar way, I must say to my patients, "Give me your worries, give me your cares. I don't allow you to worry." When we've turned our lives over to God, we can also take on the burdens of others and give them to the Lord. We give others freedom as they cast their anxieties on us.

Intercessory prayer is demanding and exhausting. At St. Luke's, it also is a way of life. I spend a lot of time reassuring patients that I care about them and that the specialists at St. Luke's are committed to handling all of their concerns. But reassurance is meaningless without prayer. We offer to pray for all patients before surgery and at any

time they request. Those prayers change the way
patients feel and the way staff members feel.

As we pray with our patients, one of the most important things we do is to pray that the Person of Jesus
Christ will be near to them. It is another way of asking
that the Holy Spirit will work in their hearts and that the
Father will bless them individually.

Recently, I sent a memo to our St. Luke's staff. I said,
"Prayer with patients must start with the way we think.
It must be centered in our thought processes as our
hearts are inclined to the Lord." It went on to say:

> Prayer with our patients should be asking God for
> His blessings upon them. We should think of the
> Lord and pray for His blessing upon each patient.
> That's the essence of the intercessory prayer we
> should make as providers of health care who are
> committed to God.
>
> As each of you cares for patients, I would like
> you to think of wishing them God's blessings and
> many benefits. I refer to it as I talk to our
> patients. I don't say a formal prayer. I say, "I wish
> you many benefits and blessings from the sur-
> gery." While speaking, I am thinking that in my
> head and wishing them God's blessings. I think
> this is the best, simplest and soundest way to
> approach prayer.
>
> The quiet, loving and "motherly approach of
> caring" is the Christian way to present patients
> with the healing intent. The "caring for" is the
> absolute essential—to truly care to give God's
> blessings to each of our patients. It is most impor-
> tant that in our heart we are in prayer to God;
> that the inclinations of our heart are toward Him
> as we care for patients.
>
> It is essential, and as a foundation to prayer for
> patients, that we must be in prayer not only to the
> Lord once, or many times, or constantly
> throughout the day, but we must be in prayer

with our spouse and family. We must break down the hedges that prevent us from praying with our loved ones and blessing them. Every morning I get on my knees and ask God to forgive me of my sins; to let me be totally surrendered throughout the day and to keep me from being an arrogant physician. I pray with my spouse, touching her, and I ask God to bless her. I pray for every part of her. She says that our prayers have held us together and have made our relationship even more beautiful than ever before.

If you have any thoughts on prayer with patients, I would greatly appreciate them. If you want to sit down and talk, I am open and available at all times. Come to me if you have some thoughts that can help me, can help you, can help other people, and particularly, can help our patients as we keep focused on the Redeemer in our prayer life, in our work life, and in everything we do.

It doesn't make any difference at St. Luke's where a person is in his or her walk with the Lord. We try to meet them on the journey and let every patient know that we understand and want to help. For some people, the issue is one of trust. Many patients don't trust anybody—not the doctors and especially not the Lord. Through Scripture readings and prayer, I try to help them understand that without trust, we cannot help them.

Patients frequently have mixed feelings about prayer. But when they come to me, they want prayer. As the nurses pray for each patient in surgery or as I pray for a patient, the purpose is to look into the patient's eyes and then pray to the Redeemer so our concerns are those of the patient. But the direction of our hearts and our voices is to the Lord. It is important for me to remember that patients pick up on whatever is happening in my daily life. If I am agitated or angry, they realize that and become more nervous. Praying and studying God's Word help provide me with the disposition to be God's healing hands.

I encourage all my staff members to pray realistically. Being absurd about prayer makes a mockery of religion. At St. Luke's, we pray for God's will. We are careful not to overwhelm patients.

Most of my prayers with patients are of thanks. I thank the patients for their faith in the Lord and for trusting me as their physician. But mostly, I thank the Lord for leading them to me. Prayers of thanksgiving help me to overcome my desire for self-sufficiency as a physician and help me turn over the responsibility for the ultimate healing to the Ultimate One—Jesus Christ.

Intercession is the backbone of most people who are prayer warriors. They pray for other people—for their strength and well-being. They are characteristically self-less people. Intercession is much of what prayer is about. That selfless attitude of giving control over to God and seeking His will is the inner disposition each of us should seek in our relationship with our Redeemer.

PRAYER IN ACTION

CHAPTER ELEVEN: JOY IN THE WORKPLACE

For group discussion or personal reflection:

1. Do you have a symbol of your faith in God in your workplace? Why or why not?

2. What are some practical ways you could bring God into your workplace and your work life?

3. Can you be focused in your walk with God and still give your work the attention it deserves?

4. How does your work glorify God?

5. The fruit of the Spirit is love, joy, peace, patience, kindness, goodness, faithfulness, gentleness and self-control. How do you exhibit these at work?

6. Do you pray for your colleagues? Do you pray for them openly at work? How do you tell them you're praying for them?

7. What are the roadblocks you face in trying to live a lifestyle of prayer at work?

CHAPTER TWELVE

TRANSFORMED BY PRAYER

When we are consumed by our relationship in prayer with the Lord, our lives are changed. If we are in God and God is within us, our meditation changes us because God takes over more of us. When our whole being is in prayer with God and we feel His peace and joy within us, the way we live our lives has to be different.

God has the power to change all of us. The Bible is full of stories of lives changed by God. Shy Moses became a great leader of the Israelites (Exodus 3 and 4). The fanatical persecutor Saul was transformed into a globe-trotting apostle (Acts 9:1–31). In the same way, our Redeemer has the power to change us from self-centered, callous people into loving, caring followers of His Word who are filled with His Spirit.

The changes in our lives may not happen so dramatically or quickly. Yet just as these men saw God's glory revealed, so do we. They may have seen it in a burning bush or heard God speak on the road to Damascus. God may reveal His glory to us as we build our relationship through prayer.

"Prayer has the power to transform your entire existence," says Dr. Juan Batlle of the Dominican Republic. "Nothing is beyond the influence of prayer. The impossible is made possible, the incurable is made curable, life and death are defied by prayer and there is no force strong enough to resist its strength."

As our personal lives of prayer progress from glory to glory and as we discover what it really means to be aligned with God, the Holy Spirit will bring forth fruit in us—love, joy, peace, patience, kindness, goodness, faithfulness, gentleness and self-control.

And that fruit shows itself through our service. Effective Christian service flows from a heart that acknowledges the glory, majesty and power of One who is King yet came to serve. When that desire for service flows through us, we won't have to force ourselves to do God's will. Dead obedience falls by the wayside. Our spirit will radiate the joy of salvation in all that we think and do, and we won't get tired of doing God's will. As Nehemiah 8:10 says, "For the joy of the Lord is your strength."

As such joy grows in us, cultivated by our relationship of prayer with our Redeemer, we experience new freedom. No longer do the anxieties and fears of this world bind us. No longer do we struggle to satisfy our own desires or impress others.

We have the freedom to give our fears, our worries and our problems to God. And we then abide in Him, knowing through faith He will provide for us because He loves us. Our relationship with God through prayer is a limitless supply of peace and joy that fills us today, tomorrow and for eternity.

PART THREE

POWER IN PRAYER

CHAPTER THIRTEEN

PRACTICING MEDICINE
AND PRAYER

W e've talked about how prayer changes our lives, how it brings us closer to God and aligns our will with His. Prayer plays a key role in my professional life and in the lives of my colleagues because as doctors, we face a unique challenge and opportunity to bring prayer to the workplace—we can pray for and with our patients.

"Truly, I feel prayer is the real heart of medicine," says Dr. Al Thomas of Hot Springs, Arkansas. "Practicing medicine without prayer becomes hollow and shallow as compared to ministering to patients with a whole-person medicine approach with the aid of the Lord Jesus Christ."

"I have learned to value the power of prayer and its significance in bringing the patient and family, the nurses, the students and the physician closer together and closer to our Lord Jesus Christ," says Dr. Juan Batlle. "This wonderful relationship has changed in such a deep way my practice of medicine that I feel that those that do not know of its power of significance are truly missing out on one of the most profound joys of our profession."

"Before I go into surgery, I always pause and humble myself before God and ask Him to make these patients see extremely well again," says Dr. Elizabeth Vaughn of Dallas. "To have an ease in doing beautiful, uncomplicated surgery is definitely a gift from God."

"God does not really need our surgery to provide healing to the patients but allows us the opportunity to serve in the Kingdom, to rectify illness and disease, and

allows us the enthusiasm to share His love and conse-
quent healing," says Dr. James Rowsey of St. Luke's
Cataract and Laser Institute.

Dr. J. Lawton Smith of Miami lists six reasons doctors
should pray with their patients: because God answers
prayer; because of love and compassion for the patients;
to serve as a witness; to get help in diagnosis and man-
agement decisions; to make medical and surgical efforts
more effective; and because everyone is scripturally commanded to pray.

"The bottom line, therefore, of why we should pray for
our patients is that if we have faith in the living God and
obey Him, God will answer our prayers," Dr. Smith says.
"There is no greater faith builder in this world that I
know of than to see open, direct and unconditional
answers to prayer."

CHAPTER FOURTEEN

PRAYING TOGETHER

Apatient was referred to Dr. James Rowsey for treatment. He saw the doctor and agreed to the course of action, and then Dr. Rowsey asked whether he could pray with him before the surgery. He and his family said yes. After the prayer, the patient told Dr. Rowsey that the previous doctor had said, "I would like to forewarn you that Dr. Rowsey is a peculiar doctor. He will probably ask you if he can pray for you before doing surgery. Don't be afraid of the prayer; this is Dr. Rowsey's way."

The patient told that doctor he could have given Dr. Rowsey no higher recommendation. He told Dr. Rowsey that he and his family considered themselves "peculiar people" in love with Jesus. "The mention of Jesus' name brings power both to the patient and to the physician," Dr. Rowsey says.

THE PRESENCE OF THE LORD

My colleagues have shared their thoughts about prayer—for themselves and for others. They all agree they must be faithful, fervent and focused in their individual prayer lives before they can pray for their patients. This helps them keep aligned with God as they do His work during their day. Doctors have to relate to people in an anointed, prayerful attitude. The prayers should be those of thanks and blessings for the patient, of guidance as we practice medicine and of love, so doctors are truly compassionate and caring.

"Our prayer life within our practice is no different from our prayer life outside the practice," says Dr. Tom

Goodgame of Palm Harbor, Florida. "Our communications with God are a constant part of our preparation for both technical and interpersonal enterprises."

A consistent prayer life, doctors say, helps them remember their mission as they serve others.

"I view everyone who walks into my office as being sent by God so that He can care for them with excellence and compassion," says Dr. Elizabeth Vaughn. "I like to treat each patient as though that patient is Jesus Christ... the individual person I am seeing deserves to be treated just as carefully and with as high a level of excellence as I would treat Jesus Christ were He sitting in my examining chair."

"As I walk into the office I will audibly or sometimes quietly pray that the Lord will fill this small 1,200-square-foot office with his presence," says Dr. James A. Avery.

"We pray because the physician is limited to prescribing or applying a treatment, but is never able to control its effectiveness," says Dr. Ralph Johnson of St. Petersburg, Florida. "If one accepts the hypothesis that the healing effects of treatment depend upon God's grace, intercession becomes mandatory. For to not intercede replaces dependence upon God with dependence on self, thereby in a sense violating the First Commandment."

Prayer is not a last resort—a time to recognize defeat or desperation. A doctor who was a self-proclaimed atheist visited Dr. Juan Batlle in the Dominican Republic. When he saw Dr. Batlle and his staff gather for their daily devotional and prayer for their patients, he questioned their confidence in their skills. He said, facetiously, "Hey, I didn't know that your surgical skill was so bad that you had to pray for help before the day began." To this doctor, prayer was failure, not the opportunity to reaffirm an allegiance with God or submission to His will so His healing could be accomplished.

One major benefit Dr. James A. Avery sees of praying with patients is that prayer increases the bonding between the patient and the physician. "I have seen patients who come in bitter and angry at doctors in general literally melt after prayer and become some of the most trusting patients," he says. "It is a great mystery to me, but one person genuinely reaching out to God for another is a remarkable phenomenon that we take too lightly."

Praying With Patients

These doctors believe in the power of praying with patients. Their prayers may take several forms, but prayer is an active part of their work.

"I pray aloud with clients most often at the end of each session," says Dr. Dennis Cox, a Christian counselor. Dr. Cox thanks the Lord for His presence and guidance during the session, asking for His courage to put what was learned during the session into practice. Dr. Cox also has started praying more with clients at the beginning of the session, dedicating the hour to the Lord.

"Many are extremely tense and confused when they first come to the session," Dr. Cox says, "and praying with them reminds them that God is there and will help them to relate to me what needs to be spoken." Dr. Cox says that when he prays out loud the clients are Christians and welcome the prayer. "It has always had an encouraging effect on the client to turn to God with me for help when the situation seems so far beyond human control. Such times remind us that our ultimate hope must always be in God and not in man. Yet our prayer reminds us that God's help is always available."

Dr. Batlle says "farewell prayers" adapt well to busy medical practices. He offers a few words, such as "May God bless you" or "May Jesus fill your life," to patients as they leave the office. "These farewell prayers leave your patients with a clear perception of the pureness of the advice or counsel that has been given." Sometimes patients are surprised or a little confused at first, but they learn to appreciate the prayers, Dr. Batlle says. "Some patients get to the point of requesting these few words of prayer when their doctor forgets to offer them," he says.

Mickey Evans, of the Dunklin Memorial Camp in Okeechobee, Florida, says, "I have been amazed in the difference that prayer makes...Conventional prayer— bow your head, close your eyes—seems to make little impact on people who are certainly not in a prayerful mode when they come into my office. But when I just begin conversational prayer, making eye contact briefly with each family member as I pray, the atmosphere changes as we invite His peace and presence to be manifested in our encounter."

Evans says this form of prayer requires spiritual receptivity from the counselor as well as clients and family. "But when we allow the Lord to work in us both 'to will and to act according to his good purpose' (Philippians 2:13), His Spirit will flow out of our innermost being and minister to people's needs in a way that our medical knowledge and counseling skills could never touch."

I am careful when I pray with patients to avoid doing anything unrealistic or sensational. The faith that I have as a doctor has to be a sufficient example to my patients. I am reminded often in my prayers that I have to be quiet and firm and not offensive to patients.

Christians have a particular call to be sure we do not come off as more righteous than others. Individuals who are not authentic or accountable in the Christian pursuits could damage our credibility in the eyes of the world. As a Christian medical practitioner, I am aware of much that takes place in the name of healing that is not Scriptural. I have faith that any of these movements not of Jesus will eventually fall apart.

Approaching Patients About Prayer

Dr. Elizabeth Vaughn says her patients are appreciative when she prays for them, seeking God's help and intervention in their problems. "Sometimes when people seem so distraught over their situation, I ask them if they would like for me to pray with them. I can't remember anyone ever declining."

One patient in particular was very apprehensive about her surgery. "When I asked her if she would like me to pray, she said, 'It seems like I have asked everyone else's opinion, and I never even thought to take it to God.'" Vaughn says, "She was very grateful that we had incorporated Him into her solution and asked Him to heal her eye."

Dr. James Rowsey says, "Some truly enjoyable experiences have occurred as God has continued to heal me at the same time He heals patients." Dr. Rowsey says he was nervous and hesitant when he first began praying with patients and wondered how they would respond when he talked with them about prayer.

One time, he was examining a motorcycle gang member whose vision could be improved by surgery. "As I was explaining the details of the required surgery, I glanced casually at his leather pants, chain belt, sleeveless T-shirt and numerous arm tattoos and realized that prayer would be potentially inappropriate." He was worried that if the man objected, he might throw Dr. Rowsey into the hallway and leave. The man's brother, who was similarly dressed, was in the examination room as Dr. Rowsey explained the risks and benefits of surgery.

"I recall asking the Lord in my heart, 'Lord, are you sure you want me to pray for this man? How about skipping this one?' The Lord was faithful, however, to my obedience to His desire to have prayer in my practice."

Dr. Rowsey put his hand on the patient's arm, asked whether he had any other questions and said he could place the man's name on the corneal transplant list. Dr. Rowsey continued, telling the man, "Before I recommend surgery on anyone, however, I would like to ask your permission to pray for you. I am in the surgery business, but the Lord Himself is in the healing business."

The man's response surprised Dr. Rowsey. He said he would be delighted if the doctor would pray for him. About halfway through the first sentence of the prayer, the man's brother responded: "Hallelujah, Jesus. We thank You for sending us to a Christian doctor." The patient also began to pray: "Thank You, Lord, for allowing us to be with one of Your men so that I can see again."

After the prayer was over, the two men told Dr. Rowsey that while they were members of a motorcycle gang they were born again and filled with the Holy Spirit. They realized the other members of the gang would believe the witness of these two brothers more than the witness of outsiders, so their ministry was dedicated to presenting Jesus to this group. "I was thoroughly astounded by God's grace and perseverance and over-joyed by the presence that God provided from my own obedience," Dr. Rowsey says.

GETTING PATIENTS TO PRAY

Psychologist James B. Morris says he works with Christian patients to find the causes of their anger, unforgiveness, resentment and other problems. When the time is right, he encourages patients to repent of harmful attitudes and seek God's help and forgiveness—all of which are essential steps in the healing process. "I encourage them to pray about these matters throughout the day and to enlist a faithful prayer partner who will intercede for them," Dr. Morris says. "Not only does this practice tend to strengthen the believer's relationship with the Lord, but it brings about remarkable change in his life and attitude."

A patient of Dr. Morris showed such a turnaround.

Susan had been in a serious car accident in which two of the passengers in her car were killed. Susan also was seriously injured, and her recovery was slow and painful. A year after the crash, she still had headaches, leg and back pain and other frequent ailments. She was constantly depressed, had lost her enthusiasm about everything and was overprotective of her children. Finally she was referred to Dr. Morris.

"During our sessions, Susan spoke angrily of the careless young woman who had caused the accident," Dr. Morris says. "In effect, she said, 'That young girl didn't even come over to help us or even to speak, but just stood around smoking as the ambulances and helicopters took us to the hospitals.'"

In addition to being angry with the other driver, Susan also felt guilty about the deaths of her passengers, even though she wasn't at fault in the accident. Her guilt made her feel as though she had no right to good health or happiness.

"I began to point out the irrationality of her guilt feelings," Dr. Morris says. "I reminded Susan that God is sovereign, and while we may not understand the pain of such a tragedy, we are assured that even in this, God works for our good." Susan's depression, anger and guilt began to diminish. Her interest in life returned. Through prayer Susan was restored.

BEING LED TO PRAY

Dr. James Avery says he doesn't pray for every patient, and he doesn't know how he decides for which patients he'll pray. "Some patients do ask me to pray for them, and I always oblige," he says. "At other times, the Holy Spirit definitely tugs at my heart and guides me into a prayer. Sometimes I do not have a solution to a patient's problem, and I will pray with the patient for God's intervention."

And doctors don't always pray verbally with every patient. "Circumstances will often suggest the preferable way of coming to God in prayer," Dr. Ralph Johnson says. "I believe that verbal prayer which allows for, if not encourages, the participation of others present should be the general rule when the patient is a believer." Among non-believers, he says, even a casual comment such as "There are so many people praying for John's recovery" will create an opportunity for verbal prayer.

"The willingness of physicians to witness their dependence upon God is very rarely objectionable to patients," he says. "To the contrary, it is frequently a great solace. And even when adversity toward our Creator is expressed, there should always be silent intercession made for our patients. For God is merciful and has never confined His healing grace to believers."

BEYOND THE DOCTOR'S OFFICE

Prayers don't stop when the doctors close up their offices at the end of the business day. "My prayer life goes beyond the actual sessions," Dr. Dennis Cox says. "I try to pray for each of my clients, though the cases that trouble me get most of my attention. I bring up each name and face and review before the Lord what I have done."

Dr. Cox asks for God's wisdom, courage and power to help his clients, but he also uses prayer for his own emotional balance. "A good prayer life is the foundation of openness with others, because once we have shared ourselves with Him, we can better know what to share with others.

"This openness is especially important and yet difficult for counselors, because we often have to override our own feelings in order to enter into the feelings of others. Our days are filled with conversations about pain, and if we have nowhere to go with that pain, we can easily wear out ourselves. Prayer is one important place to go with that pain."

One Doctor's Story

Dr. Ralph E. Johnson, a father of four and grandfather of six, came to Florida seventeen years ago to open a new cancer center at Bayfront Medical Center in St. Petersburg. He had been head of radiation and therapy at the National Cancer Institute in Bethesda, Maryland. Bayfront didn't realize, he says, that he had a serious drinking problem. About ten years ago, his lifestyle caught up with him.

"I lost everything I had," he says. "I lost my family, my profession and my practice—right up to the point of no return."

He attended a Cursillo retreat through his Episcopal church and heard testimony from a witness recovering from alcoholism. "I thought he was telling the story of my life," Dr. Johnson says. "It was just like the scales came off my eyes."

That turning point led him to ask a group of laymen to pray with him for healing. While they prayed, he says he was overcome by a "great and wonderful conviction. My addiction and everything was gone," he says. "The compulsion was just taken away."

About six years ago, he became an active, charismatic Christian. He remembers the moment of his greatest conversion: He was in his study reading the Bible, and he began "weeping before the Lord." He continued to read for six hours and all day the next day. After a month of reading the Bible every day, he began to pray with other people.

Now in his practice he prays with patients. As soon as he started praying with them, "They were being cured with no treatment," he says. "They would begin to weep and want Jesus in their lives. It was the power of the Spirit working... God began to open a mission field here."

While some local professionals and patients were skeptical of his prayers, Dr. Johnson said he found a great reception in Third World countries where he traveled with his wife Sylvia. For a time, Dr. Johnson continued with his busy medical practice, despite the fact that some physicians refused to refer patients to him because of his religious convictions. Through God's leading, Dr. Johnson began a "new career" as a volunteer chaplain in prisons in the late 1990s. Instead of using him to treat physical ailments, the Lord has lead Dr. Johnson to treat those with spiritual sickness. Teaching others to surrender fully to God has become Dr. Johnson's passion.

CHAPTER FIFTEEN

PRAYER AND HEALING

Prayers by doctors and patients may take many forms, but those prayers always rely on the power of God and faith in Him as the Creator of the universe. Some become Christians by contact with a doctor who prays. And many feel the Holy Spirit comforting them during the stressful times that medical procedures bring. Perhaps one of the most visible ways these prayers manifest themselves is through healing. That healing can take many forms but has one common element—faith in the Lord Jesus Christ.

Too many people, including many physicians, try to reason with the Lord and make Him a matter of reason. They say the only way we can get from the natural to the supernatural is through reason. They may not believe in God's power, which manifests itself in various forms of healing. But we cannot always find ways in the natural world to explain healing. It isn't reason; it must be through faith that we see God's power. When religion becomes all reason, it loses its supernatural content.

One example we have of such faith is the healing of Jairus' daughter. Luke 8:49–56 tells the story:

> While Jesus was still speaking, someone came from the house of Jairus, the synagogue ruler. "Your daughter is dead," he said. "Don't bother the teacher any more."
>
> Hearing this, Jesus said to Jairus, "Don't be afraid; just believe, and she will be healed."
>
> When he arrived at the house of Jairus, he did not let anyone go in with him except Peter, John and James, and the child's father and mother. Meanwhile, all the people were wailing and

mourning for her. "Stop wailing," Jesus said. "She is not dead but asleep."

They laughed at him, knowing that she was dead. But he took her by the hand and said, "My child, get up!" Her spirit returned, and at once she stood up. Then Jesus told them to give her something to eat. Her parents were astonished, but he ordered them not to tell anyone what had happened.

Faith and faithfulness are part of what healing is about. When we have faith in the power of the Holy Spirit, there is healing. Mark 5:25–34 gives us another example of faith and healing:

And a woman was there who had been subject to bleeding for twelve years. She had suffered a great deal under the care of many doctors and had spent all she had, yet instead of getting better she grew worse. When she heard about Jesus, she came up behind him in the crowd and touched his cloak, because she thought, "If I just touch his clothes, I will be healed." Immediately her bleeding stopped and she felt in her body that she was freed from her suffering.

At once Jesus realized that power had gone out from him. He turned around in the crowd and asked, "Who touched my clothes?"

"You see the people crowding against you," his disciples answered, "and yet you can ask, 'Who touched me?'"

But Jesus kept looking around to see who had done it. Then the woman, knowing what had happened to her, came and fell at his feet and, trembling with fear, told him the whole truth. He said to her, "Daughter, your faith has healed you. Go in peace and be freed from your suffering."

When the woman touched Jesus' cloak, power went out from him. That power represents the Holy Spirit working through Jesus. The New Testament word for power is *dunamis,* and that power is available to all believers. We must embrace the living Word of God—Jesus Christ—to tap into His healing power. The Reverend Jack Taylor, in his book *The Word of God With Power*, writes that there must be an acting in us through the Holy Spirit to receive power.

There are two important points about healing. First, all healing comes from God. It may be healing He set in motion in the physical world, when our bodies are healed of disease; it may be what we view as miraculous healing. Or it may not be physical healing at all, but spiritual healing. Second, while we look at healing from our short-term perspective of life on earth, God has an eternal view of healing. Frequently we are healed as we're taken to heaven.

The Reverend J.I. Packer says Joni Eareckson Tada, who is paralyzed from the neck down, is one of the most spiritually healthy people he knows. Some would pity her because of her physical condition. But the most important health is our spiritual health. Then comes our physical health.

"The power of prayer in our practice is not a power which we use," Dr. Tom Goodgame says. "It is a power which uses us. We must constantly remind ourselves that our objective is not to bend God's will so that it conforms to ours, but instead to continually try to change our lives to better conform to His will for us."

Five Types of Healing

Does that mean if we have enough faith we will always be healed? As I saw a friend battle cancer, I learned more about God and healing. My friend, Jamie Buckingham, had a difficult time accepting that he had cancer. During his year-and-a-half-long battle, through all the tests and operations and other medical procedures, he kept asking the Lord what He was trying to tell Jamie. He waged a valiant fight, enjoyed a series of miracles, but then he died.

Was he really healed? Absolutely. Jamie learned, and taught me, that the Lord was saying it was time for the two of them to get closer. It was time for Jamie to get rid of any excess baggage—his church and work obligations—and let it be just Jesus and Jamie, Jamie and Jesus.

Jamie was on a "new high" at a time when some would have given up. He was more acutely aware of God's presence, and life became more meaningful for him—especially his relationships with other people. As I see it, he experienced five distinct types of healing. Here is how I believe God uses each type:

1. Natural Healing

When you cut your finger, get a cold or bruise your leg you get the chance to see natural healing. God, the ultimate designer, organized our bodies to take care of themselves in a normal reaction to injury. The Bible tells us that we need to depend upon God and not on ourselves through our physical and spiritual illnesses. Psalm 30:2 says, "O Lord my God, I called to you for help and you healed me."

We take this natural healing for granted. But it's due to the miracle of a very wise Creator, who designed a countless number of microscopic cells to fulfill their own unique purpose. Praise to our Creator, who designed our body with spontaneous healing ability.

2. Assisted Healing

The Lord has given us the wisdom and knowledge to heal. When we use that wisdom and knowledge, or rely on those who use it, we can be healed. All knowledge is God-given, but it is implemented by people—even unbelievers. All the information He created is used to treat us when we are sick. And as we understand His creation, we pass that information along. We teach it; we put it in text-books so others may learn. So the knowledge a good doctor has, regardless of whether he is a believer, comes from God. Knowledge can lead you to a good doctor who can treat you.

Doctors who pray know the power of assisted healing. "I pray for God to give me wisdom when I make decisions regarding patients' diagnoses and treatment," Dr. Ronald Haynes says. "When I assist on a surgical case, I pray for God to guide the surgeon's hand."

Dr. Elizabeth Vaughn says she also asks the Lord to intervene in complicated situations. "I stand amazed at how beautifully He works out a very difficult predica-ment," she says. "When the Lord shows me in surgery how to do things I've never seen, it is like putting your foot all the way down on an accelerator and feeling the car lunge into a high speed. It is a new dimension of wisdom that you know came from God and not from yourself."

Dr. Dennis Cox prays inaudibly during therapy ses-sions with clients. "Whenever I am unsure of where to go or whenever I sense resistance on the part of the client, I pray for God's intervention to move us all along the proper path in the session."

My friend Jamie used wisdom and knowledge to receive a doctor's help. He used wisdom to get radiation treatments. But most of all, he used wisdom as he real-ized the importance of his relationship with Jesus. It's important that we use that wisdom in our approach to healing. We cannot be purely emotional or purely spiri-tual; otherwise, we will see Christ only in showmanship. We must see Him in everything we do. So we must be bal-anced and mature in our relationship with Christ. A mature relationship means we'll have a wise approach to healing. It means we'll know that physical healing is important and we'll seek it, but more important will be our spiritual healing. Whether or not we become physically healed, we'll become spiritually healed.

3. *Miraculous Healing*

Miracles have occurred since the beginning of the ages and still occur. Some say miracles were different during Jesus' time than they are now, and that's probably true. But miracles certainly exist now. When a patient does better than expected, many professionals say it's "very unusual." It's more than that; it's a miracle.

We see many people healed who we didn't think would be. And we claim a miracle. What we must do, however, is have faith that a miracle will occur, along with seeking wise medical care. Of course, we have faith that a miracle will occur. But we must take a mature approach to healing and know that God works through doctors and nurses as well as through miracles.

4. *Inner Healing*

Spiritual illness can weigh us down just as physical illness can. When we are out of tune with God's will, when His desires are not our desires, we need healing. We must align ourselves with Him if we are going to live the life the Lord wants us to live. He seeks our wholeness through a close relationship with Him.

God's Word tells us that we need to be transformed and aligned in a Christlike way to be healed spiritually as well as physically:

> Therefore I urge you, brothers, in view of God's mercy, to offer your bodies as living sacrifices, holy and pleasing to God—this is your spiritual act of worship. Do not conform any longer to the pattern of this world, but be transformed by the renewing of your mind. Then you will be able to test and approve what God's will is—his good, pleasing and perfect will.
>
> ROMANS 12:1–2

Unless we are aligned with His will, He won't heal us in His normal fashion—the first type of healing we discussed. Nothing short of total dependence of our will, and repentance of our sins, will do. If we are angry or bitter or full of lusts or unforgiveness, we will never have the abundant life God wants us to have. And as we shed more of those desires, we will grow closer to the Lord.

Like athletes training to win a race, we are faithful, fervent and focused on our Redeemer and His will for us. Then we can rely on His strength to overcome these obstacles. We become integrated with the Lord. Our mind is full of the Word, our will is controlled by the Holy Spirit, our emotions are filled with Jesus and we love Him because of our belief. As we focus more and more on this deepening relationship, physical healing loses its attraction.

5. *Spiritual Freedom*

This is the "new high" my friend Jamie experienced. Frequently, we have so much of a worldview that we don't recognize the ultimate healing—that of being with our Redeemer in heaven. Jamie was relieved from the fear of death and walked closer to the Lord than ever. Jesus' resurrection obliterates the fear of death for us. Paul writes eloquently of this freedom from the fear of death in 1 Corinthians 15:54–55, 57:

> When the perishable has been clothed with the imperishable, and the mortal with immortality, then the saying that is written will come true. "Death has been swallowed up in victory."
> "Where, O death, is your victory? Where, O death, is your sting?"
> But thanks be to God! He gives us the victory through our Lord Jesus Christ.

This is the ultimate healing; it's actually a cure, and one that is permanent. We're released from our works. We're released from our sins. It's just Jesus and us. He's the only permanent cure for what ails us.

I believe that disease and trials in our lives bring us closer to the Lord. They make us humble and make us run to Him. My job as a Christian is to help individuals on that journey of becoming closer to God through the crosses they are given. I can serve as a caregiver, encouraging patients to give their care to me and to the Lord. I believe in miracles and healings. But I believe they are rare. The greatest miracles I have seen are those that result in lives that are changed through faith in God.

CHAPTER SIXTEEN

WITNESSES TO GOD'S POWER

In the last chapter, we discussed five types of healing. Now let's look at some examples of how these types of healing have been manifested in the lives of doctors and their patients.

GOD PROVIDES THE TOOLS

God provides solutions to difficult problems. A patient of Dr. James Rowsey needed a large corneal transplant, but Dr. Rowsey was missing a piece of equipment, an 18 mm trephine, to perform the surgery. As he traveled from Oklahoma City to Amarillo, Texas for a meeting, he prayed for a solution to the patient's problem.

At breakfast the next morning, Dr. Rowsey happened to be seated next to Dr. Eduardo Arenas, who was a specialist in the kind of transplant the patient needed. The doctor reviewed his surgical techniques for Dr. Rowsey so that "it would be quite easy to accomplish the procedure." Dr Rowsey says, "The only thing missing was the 18 mm trephine to be able to accomplish the task. Eduardo reached into his briefcase and stated, 'I decided to bring one with me to the United States in case someone needed it.'" As the Lord says in Jeremiah 33:3, "Call to me and I will answer you and tell you great and unsearchable things you do not know." "Medicine is far more exciting with God's peace, Jesus' presence, and the Holy Spirit's power," Dr. Rowsey says.

A MIRACULOUS TURNAROUND

Dr. Ralph Johnson tells the story of a "trumpet call" to intercede for another. While Dr. Johnson was attending a

Sunday evening service at church in St. Petersburg, Florida, the pastor asked the congregation to pray for Phil Fairclough, an alcoholic who was in a coma and not expected to live through the night. Dr. Johnson hurried to the hospital and went to the intensive care unit to see the thirty-four-year–old man.

The nurse was discouraged, telling Dr. Johnson that Mr. Fairclough's vital signs were falling and that the attending physician had told the family to expect his death within hours. "At first, I found myself responding to the nurse's pessimism by telling her the story of Jesus restoring life to the dead Lazarus," Dr. Johnson says. "The fact that I had never verbally repeated this story to anyone in my life scarcely seemed unusual. I was merely explaining in faith that the God in whom I believed was undaunted by death, let alone a simple coma." Then he took Mr. Fairclough's hand in his.

"I was beseeching our heavenly Father to come down in glory and give a healing touch to this desperately ill young man who had lived a self-destructive life," Dr. Johnson says. The nurse seemed shaken and told Dr. Johnson that she also had "a problem with alcohol." Dr. Johnson witnessed to her about God healing his alcoholism years earlier.

About twenty minutes later, Mr. Fairclough's mother came into the ICU. She said, "Phil is looking at us." The nurse then told Dr. Johnson that within minutes of his intercessory prayer, Mr. Fairclough's eyes had started to straighten out and focus. "God had come down in His glory and with power to restore this dying non-believer to consciousness." Mr. Fairclough became a believer three days later and two days after that walked out of the hospital without assistance and went to a ranch for addicts in Lake Okeechobee, Florida.

GOD'S GRACE

One of Dr. J. Lawton Smith's "faith builders" came after

a sixty-six-year-old man underwent a successful eye operation in his clinic. After the surgery, the patient went into atrial fibrillation in the recovery room and had to be hospitalized in the cardiac intensive care unit.

Dr. Smith remembered that he had prayed verbally with the patient before surgery in the company of his wife and two other relatives. He continued to pray in confidence for the patient's well-being. The man's heart rhythm returned to normal the same day and he was discharged from the hospital the following afternoon.

The unbeliever might credit this to a lucky treatment, but Dr. Smith says, "The believer who has seen scores of such prayers answered promptly and openly can only thank the living God for another bountiful measure of His grace."

Helping the Blind to See

Dr. Lowell A. Gess, an ophthalmologist in Minnesota, has hope even in "hopeless" situations. "What and how much must be told to the patient and family (when surgery goes badly)... the stark reality of such a condition is best tempered in the early period," Dr. Gess says.

"By faith and intercessory prayer, relatively 'hopeless' conditions have improved. I feel it is 'wicked' to ever leave a patient without 'hope.' God is great and can do and has done, wonderful things," he says. "If there be any praise, let it go to Calvary."

When Dr. Gess was in the medical mission field of Africa, he operated on Kombe, who was totally blinded with mature cataracts. While Dr. Gess was waiting for the anesthetic to take effect, he talked with Kombe. "Out of the blue, I asked him if he had his choice, would he rather be a 'new creature in Christ' or have his vision restored?" With only a slight pause, he picked "a new creature in Christ." Dr. Gess says no one in the operating room really believed him; they knew Kombe was being respectful, as he was being treated in a Christian hospital. Then, after a short pause, he added, "But I want to see again, too."

The surgery on Kombe was successful, and he walked out of Dr. Gess' life. A year later, Dr. Gess was a guest speaker at a church service. As communion was being served he saw someone looking up at him who was wearing glasses—an unusual sight in a far-off place. "And then he smiled," Dr. Gess says. "My heart leaped within me. I was looking into the face of Kombe. He really meant it when he said he desired to become a new creature in Christ."

Kombe had committed his life to the Lord when he returned to his village after the eye surgery. He became a member of the local church and was hired for a good job because he could see again.

COUNTING ON PRAYER

Physical healing does not always occur when doctors pray with patients. Dr. Ronald E. Haynes, a family practitioner in Palm Harbor, Florida, tells the story of one patient, Mr. G. For seven years, Mr. G. battled cancer. Then he suddenly developed severe diabetes, and doctors found that his new disease was secondary to a pancreatic tumor. Exploratory surgery showed that the tumor was cancerous and that it had spread. Curative surgery was not possible. He died a few months later at home.

"Mr. G. was one of the most 'up' people I have ever known," Dr. Haynes says. "He was convinced, just as I am, that prayer was very important in providing him a spirit of well-being and peace during his eight-year battle with cancer." Dr. Haynes told Mr. G. that he had been praying for him and his family, and Mr. G. was appreciative. "He believed his prayers and those of his son and others had pulled him through cancer twice. He was counting on prayer to pull him through a third time, God willing.

"His story is just one of many that have demonstrated to me the great power of prayer," Dr. Haynes says.

A DIFFERENT KIND OF VICTORY

"I believe prayer allows God to work through us to effect His will in the world," says Dr. Dan Montgomery, an ophthalmologist in Inverness, Florida.

"My sense of efficiency would have me prefer that He bypass my limited resources and get straight to the business of healing directly, but thankfully, His wisdom is greater than mine."

Dr. Montgomery found a growing mass inside the left eye of one of his patients, a woman in her sixties who had undergone a mastectomy ten years earlier. The doctor didn't know whether the new problem was related to the breast disease or was something entirely new, such as a malignant eye tumor. And treatment would be different depending on the source of the problem. Since there is no routine method for getting a biopsy of a tumor in the back of the eye, Dr. Montgomery had to rely on his clinical judgment.

"Prayer is beneficial in all situations, of course, but it is in times like these that we are left with relatively few other options in our diagnostic armamentarium," Dr. Montgomery says. "She prayed and I prayed and her church members all prayed. We prayed for guidance, for comfort and for cure."

The woman's eye finally had to be removed. "Some cynics would probably call that a failure of prayer," Dr. Montgomery says. "I disagree. Through that experience of office prayer, the patient and I were able to provide a witness to the office staff. Those brief times in the exam room before the Lord provided great comfort to the patient and left me with the sense that I was providing more total treatment, both medical and spiritual. Our subsequent post-op visits have been almost joyful times, with no apparent depression or bitterness over the loss of the eye. Prayer on her own and in the office allowed her to deal victoriously with a terrible diagnosis, a serious operation and a potentially difficult post-operative adjustment."

LIVES GIVEN TO CHRIST

Dr. James Avery also has seen patients become born-again Christians because of prayers offered for them. One woman came to his office in Clearwater with a sore throat. After Dr. Avery examined her and gave her a prescription he made a casual comment about how pretty her three-year-old daughter was. "Kathy began to cry and told me that her little girl was recently diagnosed as having leukemia and was to start chemotherapy the next week." Dr. Avery offered a very short and simple prayer that ended in tears. He then told the woman there would be no charge for the visit.

"Little did I know that Kathy had awakened that morning determined to kill herself and her daughter," Dr. Avery says. "She had whispered to a God she did not know, that if He existed, she wanted proof today 'or else.'"

That's when she got the sore throat and picked out Dr. Avery's office as the one to visit. Upon returning home after seeing Dr. Avery, she called to say she wanted to know "the God who is in that office." With the help of Dr. Avery's wife, Jan, she became an excited born-again Christian. "Only through the Holy Spirit can a simple thirty-second prayer result in a person spending eternity in heaven instead of hell!" Dr. Avery says.

Dr. Jack C. Cooper of Dallas tells about praying before surgery for one patient he understood to be a Christian. "I asked for God's blessing on us and a good result. As I was 'before the throne of grace,' I thanked the Lord for His sovereignty, for being 'on the throne of our lives—in control of our lives.'" Dr. Cooper learned something interesting a couple of weeks later, after the patient recovered. "The patient told me he thought he was a Christian until I prayed before surgery; but he became a Christian as I prayed. For the first time he realized he had been 'in control' of his life, but that was to change, for he asked Jesus to be Savior and Lord of his life— King."

LAUGHTER THERAPY

A cheerful heart is good medicine, but a crushed spirit dries up the bones.

—PROVERBS 17:22

Dr. Spencer Thornton of Nashville, Tennessee taps into the healing power of humor. "The thing that has intrigued me is the healing power of laughter itself, the physical process of laughter." The physical act of laughter lets us release some of the tension and stress we face. After we relax, we release endorphins and other body chemicals that help alleviate pain. Then we have a better outlook and attitude about life.

"One of the things that Norman Cousins pointed out in his book *Anatomy of an Illness* was that he isolated himself because the people around him couldn't stand his laughter," Thornton says. "He isolated himself and treated himself to laugh-producing stories, laugh-producing movies, and he found that after a short period, his body chemistry responded to this." To his doctors' amazement, the progress of his disease was reversed because of the way his body responded to the chemical changes laughter produced.

"One of the things we will see in the near future is experimental work showing that the act of laughter, the physical act of laughter is healing," Thornton says.

CHAPTER SEVENTEEN

A PRECIOUS POSSESSION

Training for long-distance competitions such as the Double Iron Triathalon (4.8-mile swim, 224-mile bicycle ride and 52.4-mile run) takes a long time. In my athletic career I encountered lots of ups and downs psychologically, but I found when I prayed while doing my work as an athlete, I reaped the fruit of the Spirit within me as I did athletics.

The same is true in the medical profession. The work done by my colleagues and me needs to have that same infusion of the Holy Spirit. Some people think their professional lives should be separate from their personal lives. This is absurd; both aspects of life flow together. It is the infusion of the Holy Spirit in all the elements of our lives that makes our lives meaningful and significant.

Prayer nourishes the life of God in us. It is the privilege of being co-laborers with God. It is the love of Christ flowing through us. When we prize prayer for what it is, we will use it as we ought. We need to be in a state of prayer that suggests everything depends upon God. When we are in that state, then we can communicate fully the height and depth and breadth of God's love for us and for all His children to whom we minister.

"A medical practice bathed in prayer on an hourly and daily basis is the way I feel the Lord Jesus Christ intends for us to minister to patients in medicine," Dr. Al Thomas says. "It is only by the guiding power of the Holy Spirit living within us and guiding us in our prayer life that we will be able to have a real impact on our patients as we minister to them body, soul and spirit. Only then will the cause of Jesus Christ truly be furthered to the utmost in our medical practices."

One question I often ask myself is whether I am a full-time doctor and part-time pray-er or a full-time pray-er and a part-time doctor. I believe that you have to be a full-time pray-er and a part-time doctor, part-time spouse or part-time worker in whatever you do, in order to be a balanced Christian. It is like a fish that is constantly drinking water and taking its nourishment or a bird that is constantly flying in the air. They are constantly in their worlds and doing selective things part-time.

Prayer is the key to being a balanced Christian doctor. A statement frequently made of doctors is "Work like everything depends upon us." As a physician, I often feel bruised, bent and burned-out by doing the same work all the time and dealing with personalities that sometimes are impossible to please. Therefore, I am compelled to pray. And yet, if I pray and read Scripture all day, and neglect my job or family, I will not achieve balance in my life.

When I feel the emotional gauge slip, I must turn to the Lord in prayer and let Him show me the way. I am reminded that the only one who was perfectly balanced was the Lord Jesus.

When I meet with a patient, my inner disposition should be fully of prayer, not of anxieties or worries. That prayer consumes the relationship between the patient and the doctor. Nothing else matters but the trio present—the patient, the doctor and the Lord.

When physicians get burned-out and bruised, prayer becomes even more important—so we can surrender those attitudes to God. We can be provoked by patients' complaints or anxiety or be frustrated by government regulators. But if we resent these people, we become resentful.

If we love them, we overcome what they have done. Love endures all things, and we should endure the frustrations and aggravations and respond in love to those around us. When we pray, we should pray for that kind of love.

Prayer changes us by our thanksgiving, by our rejoicing. The doctors in these pages have shared some of the many examples of lives changed by prayer—and of lives healed by prayer.

While the conditions of these doctors' patients have varied, the doctors' faith in God's love has been consistent. And they confidently turn to Him in a lifestyle of prayer. As physicians we must watch and see what the Lord will say to us, keeping our minds fixed on the Redeemer, not on what we can do.

But prayer is a pervasive force for all of us, not just doctors. We can all turn to the power of God. "When people have serious medical problems, I believe there is always someone who is praying for them," Dr. Ronald Haynes says. "It may be a close relative or friend. It may be their doctor or nurse, a respiratory therapist or physical therapist, a diet worker who brings their meal tray or a volunteer who brings their newspaper or the orderly who transports them to the X-ray department or to surgery...If the patient is not in the hospital, there is still someone praying, and if no one knows he or she is sick, there is still someone praying."

Prayer is not an exercise or show business. It is life. We battle our own independence when we turn to the Lord in prayer, seeking His help and guidance. It's unnatural; and we struggle to do it. Yet life without prayer is empty.

"For those who have led a Christian life, prayer has changed many events, circumstances, problems and situations," Dr. Juan Batlle says. "The more you pray, the more you learn to recognize its power. It is truly one of our most precious possessions."

Look to God in all things; be prayerful in all things; be aligned to Him in all things. The people who really accomplish something are the people who accomplish what the Word wants them to. The Word directs all of us to live a lifestyle of prayer. It's up to each of us to choose whether we will be faithful, fervent and focused in following the will of our Redeemer.

BENEDICTION

The following passages have been very precious in my prayer life. I hope you find them just as valuable.

Come to me, all you who are weary and burdened, and I will give you rest.

—MATTHEW 11:28

Trust in him at all times, O people; pour out your hearts to him, for God is our refuge.

—PSALM 62:8

Call upon me in the day of trouble; I will deliver you, and you will honor me.

—PSALM 50:15

Cast your cares on the LORD and he will sustain you; he will never let the righteous fall.

—PSALM 55:22

BIBLIOGRAPHY

I list here only the writings that have been of use in the making of this book. This bibliography is by no means a complete record of the works and sources I have consulted. It indicates the substance and range of reading upon which I have formed my ideas, and I intend it to serve as a convenience for those who wish to pursue the study of prayer.

BOOKS

Baxter, Richard. *The Saints' Everlasting Rest.* 1650.

Chambers, Oswald. *If You Will Ask.* 2nd ed. Nashville, TN: Discovery House Publishers, 1985.

Cornwall, Judson. *The Elements of Worship.* South Plainfield, NJ: Bridge Publishing, Inc., 1983.

Edwards, Jonathan. *A Treatise Concerning Religious Affections.* 1746.

Foster, Richard J. *Prayer: Finding the Heart's True Home.* New York: HarperCollins Publishers, 1992.

Guyon, Madame Jeanne. *Experiencing the Depths of Jesus Christ.* (Originally published as *Moyen Court et Tres Facile de Faire Oraison* or *The Short and Very Easy Method of Prayer*) 1685. Reprint, Auburn, ME: SeedSowers Christian Books Publishing House, 1975.

Hybels, Bill. *Too Busy Not to Pray: Slowing Down to Be With God.* Downers Grove, IL: InterVarsity Press. 1988.

Jennings, Theodore W. *Life as Worship.* Grand Rapids, MI: William B. Eerdmans Publishing Co., 1982.

Laubach, Frank. *Letters by a Modern Mystic*, Syracuse, NY: New Readers Press. 1979.

Laubach, Frank. *Learning the Vocabulary*, Nashville, TN:

Upper Room, 1956.

Pink, Arthur W. *Profiting From the Word*. Carlisle, PA: The Banner of Truth Trust, 1985.

Ravenhill, Leonard. *Revival Praying*. Minneapolis, MN: Bethany House Publishers, 1962.

Seamands, David A. *Freedom from the Performance Trap*. Wheaton, IL: Victor Books, 1988.

___. *Healing for Damaged Emotions*. Wheaton, IL; Victor Books, 1981.

___. *Healing of Memories*. Wheaton, IL: Victor Books, 1985.

___. *Putting Away Childish Things*. 2nd ed. Wheaton, IL: Victor Books, 1993.

Stanley, Charles. *The Wonderful Spirit Filled Life*. Nashville, TN: Oliver-Nelson Books, 1992.

ARTICLES

Gills, James P. "The Pure Essence of Healing." *Charisma* (February 1993): 86.

Golin, Mark. "A Different Kind of Love Triangle." *Prevention* 38 (1987): 80–82.

TAPES

Packer, J.I. "The Theology of Healing." Augusta, GA: Covenant Enterprises, 1984.

Stanley, Charles. "Faith That Overcomes." Atlanta, GA: In Touch Ministries.

Swindoll, Charles R. "The Healing Work of the Spirit." Fullerton, CA: First Evangelical Free Church of Fullerton, 1993.

SCRIPTURE INDEX

ABOUT THE AUTHOR

James P. Gills, M.D., is founder and director of St. Luke's Cataract and Laser Institute in Tarpon Springs, Florida. Internationally respected as a cataract surgeon, Dr. Gills has performed more cataract extractions with lens implantations than anyone else in the world. He has pioneered many advancements in the field of ophthalmology to make cataract surgery safer and easier.

As a world-renowned ophthalmologist, Dr. Gills has received innumerable medical and educational awards, highlighted by 1994–1999 listings in The Best Doctors in America. Dr. Gills is a clinical professor of ophthalmology at the University of South Florida, and was named one of the Best Ophthalmologists in America in 1996 by ophthalmic academic leaders nationwide. He serves on the board of directors of the American College of Eye Surgeons, the Board of Visitors at Duke University Medical Center, and the advisory board of Wilmer Ophthalmological Institute at Johns Hopkins University. He has published more than 170 medical papers and authored eight medical textbooks. Listed in *Marquis Who's Who in America*, Dr. Gills was Entrepreneur of the Year 1990 for the State of Florida, received the Tampa Bay Business Hall of Fame Award in 1993, and the Tampa Bay Ethics Award from the University of Tampa in 1995. In 1996 he was awarded the prestigious Innovators Award by his colleagues in the American Society of Cataract and Refractive Surgeons. In 2000 he was presented with the Florida Enterprise Medal by the Merchants Association of Florida, named Humanitarian of the Year by the Golda Meir/Kent Jewish Center in Clearwater, and Free Enterpriser of the Year by the Florida Council on Economic Education. In 2001 The Salvation Army presented to Dr. Gills their prestigious "Others" Award in honor of his lifelong commitment to service and caring.

Dr. Gills has dedicated his life to restoring much more than physical vision. He seeks to encourage and comfort the patients who come to St. Luke's. It was through sharing his insights with patients that he initially began writing on Christian topics. An avid student of the Bible for many years, he now has authored fifteen books dealing with Christian principles and physical fitness.

As an ultra-distance athlete, Dr. Gills participated in forty-six marathons, including eighteen Boston Marathons, and fourteen 100-mile mountain runs. In addition, he completed five Ironman Triathlons in Hawaii and six Double Iron Triathlons. Dr. Gills has served on the national Board of Directors of the Fellowship of Christian Athletes and in 1991 was the first recipient of their Tom Landry Award.

Married in 1962, Dr. Gills and his wife, Heather, have raised two children, Shea and Pit. Shea Gills Grundy, a former attorney now full-time mom, is a graduate of Vanderbilt University and Emory University Law School. She and husband, Shane Grundy, M.D., presented the Gills with their first grandchildren—twins, Maggie and Braddock, and three years later a third child, James Gills Grundy. The Gills' son, J. Pit Gills, M.D., ophthalmologist, received his medical degree from Duke University Medical Center and in 2001 joined the St. Luke's staff. "Dr. Pit" is married to Joy Parker-Gills. They are proud parents of Pitzer and Parker.

OTHER BOOKS BY JAMES P. GILLS, M.D.

RX FOR WORRY: A THANKFUL HEART
Discusses how each of us can find peace by resting and relaxing in the promises of God.
ISBN 0-88419-932-0

LOVE: FULFILLING THE ULTIMATE QUEST
A quick refresher course on the meaning and method of God's great gift.
ISBN 0-88419-933-9

A BIBLICAL ECONOMICS MANIFESTO
(with Ronald H. Nash, Ph.D.)
How the best understanding of economics conforms with what the Bible teaches on the subject.
ISBN 0-88419-871-5

COME UNTO ME: GOD'S CALL TO INTIMACY
Inspired by Dr. Gills' trip to the Holy Land, this book explores God's eternal desire for mankind to get to know Him intimately.
ISBN 1-59185-214-5

DARWINISM UNDER THE MICROSCOPE: HOW RECENT SCIENTIFIC EVIDENCE POINTS TO DIVINE DESIGN
Lays a scientific foundation for "divine design" and equips the reader to discuss the topic intelligently.
ISBN 0-88419-925-8

THE UNSEEN ESSENTIAL: A STORY FOR OUR TROUBLED TIMES
A compelling, contemporary novel about one man's struggle to grow into God's kind of love.
ISBN 1-879938-05-7

TENDER JOURNEY: A CONTINUING STORY FOR OUR TROUBLED TIMES
The sequel to *The Unseen Essential*.
ISBN 1-8779938-17-0

TRANSFORM YOUR MARRIAGE
An elegant 4- by 8.5-inch booklet to help couples develop new closeness with each other and with the Lord.
ISBN 1-879938-11-1

TEMPLE MAINTENANCE: EXCELLENCE WITH LOVE
A how-to book for achieving lifelong total fitness of body, mind and spirit.
ISBN 1-879938-01-4

THE DYNAMICS OF WORSHIP
Designed to rekindle the heart with a passionate love for God. Gives the who, what, when, where, why and how of worship.
ISBN 1-879938-03-0

BELIEVE AND REJOICE: CHANGED BY FAITH, FILLED WITH JOY
How faith in God can let us see His heart of joy.
ISBN 1-879938-13-8

IMAGINATIONS: MORE THAN YOU THINK
How focusing our thoughts will help us grow closer to God.
ISBN 1-879938-18-9